PRESSED FLOWERS

PRESSED FLOWERS

PAMELA LE BAILLY

David Porteous
Parkwest, New York

To Louis,
for his patience and understanding, with my love.

A CIP catalogue record for this book
is available from the British Library.

Library of Congress Catalog Card Number 96-69035

ISBN 1 870586 37 9

This paperback edition first published in the UK and
United States in 1998 by David Porteous Editions,
PO Box 5, Chudleigh,Newton Abbot, Devon, TQ13 0YZ /
Parkwest Publications, 451 Communipaw Avenue,
Jersey City, N.J., 07304.

Designed by Vic Giolitto

Printed in Hong Kong

CONTENTS

"For lo, the winter is past, the rain is over and gone;
The flowers appear on the earth."

THE SONG OF SOLOMON

INTRODUCTION

FLOWER pressing has been practised down the ages, but modern methods and materials make it possible to use pressed flowers in dozens of different ways.

I have been pressing flowers for more than 25 years, and I find the hobby just as fascinating now as I did when I first began. The excitement of finding a new flower or a leaf that changes colours or of discovering different techniques and ways to use the flowers never seems to pall. Even within a garden, individual plants can provide differently shaped and coloured flowers and leaves, and it is this enormous diversity in form, shape, texture and colour that makes flower pressing so tempting.

Everyone can start — the very young and the not so young — and only the most basic materials are needed. The smallest garden, a window box or even a tub can produce a wealth of inspiration. Walks in the country become voyages of discovery as you look at every flower and leaf with new eyes, finding unexpected shapes and sizes that you did not know existed.

One of the great joys of this craft lies in opening your press and finding the results of your work, perhaps not always as you anticipated — sometimes better, sometimes different, but always immensely satisfying — and using the flowers and leaves in some of the ways I suggest in the pages that follow. You can progress, as I did, from simple items, such as notepaper, to pictures and then to more complicated work with resin. At no stage will you ever be bored or lonely as, with tweezers in your hand and this book by your side, you enter the world of pressed flowers with all its pleasures and rewarding achievements.

1. WORKING WITH PRESSED FLOWERS

APART FROM the press itself, you will need only the simplest of tools and equipment to work with pressed flowers. You will probably have most of these items already.

The only really satisfactory adhesive for using on the backs of plant material is a rubber-based glue such as Copydex or Marvin Medium. The tubes come with a handy little pliable spatula, which I find invaluable (I sometimes buy the tubes just to get the spatula), but the larger containers are more economical. Pour a little of the adhesive into a small screw-top jar, add about 5ml (1 teaspoon) of warm water to every 30ml (2 tablespoons) of glue, screw the top down firmly and shake well. The added water makes it flow much more easily, and it dries just as well.

Beaten egg white is an excellent adhesive for very delicate petals as it does not show through, but it is not strong enough for thicker flowers or heavy stalks. It is, however, perfectly satisfactory to use when the design is going to be behind glass.

All-purpose, clear adhesives such as Uhu are useful when it comes to sticking craft work together, but they are too strong for the pressed flowers themselves.

Making a Flower Press

Some excellent flower presses can be bought in craft shops, and these consist of two boards, bolts and wing nuts and sheets of blotting-paper interleaved with corrugated card. However, as you collect more and more flowers and leaves, you will find

You will need

- ☐ flat-ended tweezers (the kind used by stamp collectors)
- ☐ craft knife
- ☐ pair of large scissors
- ☐ pair of small scissors with pointed ends
- ☐ sharp pencils
- ☐ drawing pens, sizes 01 and 02
- ☐ compass and set square
- ☐ ruler and eraser
- ☐ nylon paintbrushes, no. 07
- ☐ 2cm (¾in) paintbrush (for applying background washes)
- ☐ clear, all-purpose adhesive or egg white
- ☐ non-permanent glue stick (e.g., Tipp-ex)
- ☐ acetone
- ☐ roll of low-tack adhesive tape
- ☐ general-purpose adhesive cleaner (available from garages or motor-parts shops)
- ☐ several small jars with screw-top lids (meat-paste or mustard jars are ideal)
- ☐ Thermaseal iron-on plastic film (available from some craft outlets or photographic suppliers)
- ☐ felt-tipped pens, including gold and silver
- ☐ ball-point pens for labelling, and so on

You will need

- ☐ 2 pieces of thick plywood or chipboard, 30 × 30cm (12 × 12in)
- ☐ 4 bolts, 10–15cm (4–6in) long, and wing nuts
- ☐ sheets of smooth corrugated card, 30 × 30cm (12 × 12in)
- ☐ pieces of newspaper, 30 × 30cm (12 × 12in)
- ☐ sheets of blotting-paper, 30 × 30cm (12 × 12in)
- ☐ nappy liners
- ☐ large, good-quality paper tissues
- ☐ scissors
- ☐ cutting knife or scalpel
- ☐ pieces of plain paper, 15 × 4cm (6 × 1½in), for labelling

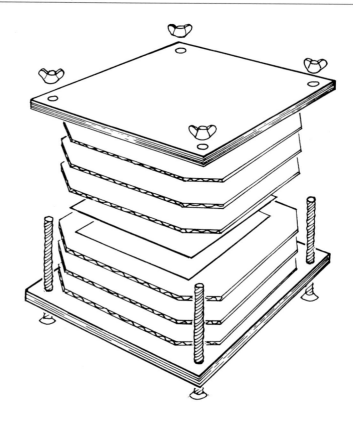

ABOVE: A flower press can be simply made from stout plywood, four bolts and pieces of card, blotting-paper and newspaper.

that you need several presses, and you can make your own very simply and cheaply.

Place the squares of plywood or chipboard together and drill a hole in all the corners of both pieces, making sure that the squares are aligned and that the holes are in exactly the same position in each so that the bolts will be straight. If you are making more than one press, mark each pair of boards A/A, B/B, C/C and so on so that you can easily match them up in future.

Insert the bolts in one of the boards. Trim the corners of the corrugated card so that the card fits inside the bolts. I cut pieces of card from strong cardboard boxes — ones that have held bottles of wine are ideal, and most supermarkets generally have spare boxes that you can take. Trim

the corners of the blotting-paper and newspaper, too. Then lay a sheet of card, four or five pieces of newspaper and a piece of blotting-paper over the board. Then lay a nappy liner over the blotting-paper — you may have to use one and a half liners to cover the whole area — and cover this with tissue, smoothing the tissue to make sure it is flat. Always use strong, 3-ply tissues and buy 'mansize' ones, which will be large enough to cover the nappy liners.

Place the flowers and leaves on the tissue and cover them with another tissue, smoothing it gently over them, then add the layers of nappy liner(s), blotting-paper and newspaper. The next layer will begin with a sheet of blotting-paper. If you are pressing thick flowers you should use a piece of card. Build up the layers to the tops

RIGHT: It is possible to buy a wide range of ready-made blanks and frames for jewellery, trinket boxes and pictures of all kinds. Make sure that your arrangements and the flowers you select are in proportion to the overall dimensions of the blank or frame.

of the bolts, adding extra layers of card at the top if necessary — you may be pressing only one or two layers, for example. Place the second board carefully in position and screw the wing nuts down, giving each nut a few turns so that you exert an even pressure on the top board. You can protect the board by placing a large washer under each wing nut. Tighten the nuts again after a few hours.

If the day feels damp, insert four or five sheets of newspaper between the cardboard and blotting-paper. Also, if you are pressing very delicate petals, use extra layers of newspaper instead of cardboard, because the corrugations in the card will mark the petals.

It is always useful to have an extra, small press that you can take with you when you go on walks in the country-side, so often a source of unexpected delights. Cut some stiff card, blotting-paper and tissue measuring 20 × 14cm (8 × 5½in). Before you go out, prepare the layers as before — card, blotting-paper, tissue, tissue, blotting-paper and card. Four or five layers are usually sufficient, and you should secure them with two strong rubber bands. Take a small pair of scissors with you. Place all the treasures you find carefully between the tissues, and as soon as you get home you can transfer the tissue layer straight to your main press without disturbing the contents.

When you are designing arrangements for small items, remember to keep to a fairly limited palette of colours. If you use too wide a range of tones or introduce strongly contrasting colours you will overwhelm the design. It is worth remembering, too, that the same flowers can look quite different when they are arranged on different coloured backgrounds.

Pressing Flowers

Always lay the flowers and leaves on the tissue. Never lay them directly on the nappy liners because they will stick to the surface of the liners and be ruined. Also, the tiny indentations in the nappy liners will mark petals and leaves. As long as they are clean, the nappy liners can be re-used. If dampness is a problem, it is advisable to change the nappy liners, blotting-paper and newspaper, but not the tissues, after a day or two.

Next, and most importantly, write the date and the names of the plants you are pressing on a label and use non-permanent adhesive to attach it to the blotting-paper. Most plants take six weeks to dry properly, and although it can be exciting to lift the layers to reveal foliage and flowers that you had forgotten about, it can be irritating to find flowers that are unidentified and unidentifiable.

Now you must leave everything for at least six weeks — some very bulky plants may take as long as eight weeks — although you can, of course, add extra material and layers to the press until it is completely full. If some of the material was damp when you placed it in the press, you can change the nappy liners and blotting-paper after a day or two. Do not change the tissue — you will disturb and damage the flowers. Everything will curl up and wrinkle if it is disturbed before a week has passed. If the weather is especially damp or if the flowers feel moist, put the whole press in the airing cupboard for two or three days.

If space is limited in the press it is quite acceptable to remove a layer of flowers after a day or two, complete with tissue, blotting-paper and so on, and store them in piles in a dry place. Allow one square of cardboard to every three or four layers of plant material and always put the newest flowers at the bottom of the pile.

When you first have a press, your first instinct is to rush out and collect everything in sight. But you must be selective. Every flower that you put in your press must be as perfect a specimen as you can find and every leaf you press must be a pretty or a useful shape. Dull and faded items do not improve miraculously in the press.

If at all possible, pick between noon and 4 o'clock in the afternoon, depending on the weather and location, of course. In very hot, sunny conditions it is advisable to pick flowers as soon as they open. If the weather is windy or damp, take polythene bags and clips or ties. Pop the plants into the bags, but make sure you do not overcrowd the contents. Blow into the bag and fasten a tie securely around the top. Most leaves and flowers will remain in pristine condition for several hours provided they are not left in the hot sun. If you pick them with a good stalk, they can be revived with a drink of water before pressing.

When you pick open flowers, cut the stalk close to the calyx and place the flower upside down on the tissue. Some flowers close up when they are picked. Gently ease them open or press them as buds. There should, as in nature, always be buds among your designs. Alternatively, you can pick them with a stalk and place them in water, when they usually open up again quite quickly.

Sprays of flowers, such as aubrietia, coral bells (*Heuchera sanguinea*) or forget-me-nots, can be pressed whole provided that any leaves or buds obscuring the flowers are removed first. Visualize the spray as you would like it to look in a design and pull off the leaves or immature flowers accordingly.

Some flowers can be split open and either pressed whole flat or divided in two. Freesias, salpiglossis and

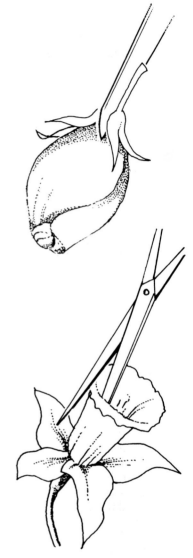

Although it is possible to press roses whole, you may prefer to press buds in two halves, which gives a pleasingly soft outline. Use a sharp knife to slice each bud in two as far as the calyx, then very gently pull the two halves apart. When you are pressing flowers such as daffodils, cut them in half and carefully press with old tissues to remove as much moisture as possible before placing them between clean tissues in your press.

alstroemeria (Peruvian lily) have lovely markings on one half of the petals; divide the flowers in two and place the veined side on top of the plain one to give depth and colour.

Provided you have a good press and really dry, sunny period, quite thick flowers such as French marigolds (*Tagetes patula*) press successfully. Cut off only part of the calyx, otherwise all the petals fall out — which is not a total disaster, because they are lovely in small designs. It is advisable to check thick flowers and to change the pressing papers after a few days.

I press roses whole because they seem to lose their depth if they are taken to pieces as many people suggest. Cut the calyx as near to the bloom as you dare. Make a small collar from two or three layers of tissue. Single roses do not need this support. Again, check for dampness after a few days, and you can, of course, place the whole press in the airing cupboard for a while to hasten the drying process if you do suspect that the plant material is damp.

Foliage such as clematis, which has tendrils or soft stalks, should be left for an hour or two to relax, to give lovely, natural curves.

Some flowers — snowdrops and scillas, for example — have really juicy stalks, which can lead to mildew or browning. Place the stalk between two layers of old tissue and press down gently, running your finger from flower head to base of stalk. You will be amazed how much liquid runs out. Repeat the process two or three times, then press. Somehow, pressing the flower and stalk separately and then putting them together in your designs never looks quite as natural.

Flowers such as poppies and love-in-a-mist have a hard seed pod in the centre. These should be removed before pressing by a gentle rocking movement, or a twist, so that the stamens are left intact.

Using Silica Gel

Some flowers are said to be impossible to press, including *Saintpaulia* (African violets) and fuchsias, because they are so full of juice that they are inclined to become brown and shapeless or to lose every vestige of colour. I used to try to squeeze the juice out of them before pressing, but even then about three-quarters of them proved to be unsatisfactory. However, I loved the deep, velvety purples so much that I kept wondering how I could manage to press the blooms and retain the colours. Then one day, when I was drying some flowers, I came across a simple solution, and now about 99 per cent of all the African violets I press are successful.

Put a layer of silica gel (which you can buy at most chemists and many craft shops) in the bottom of a plastic container with a tight-fitting lid. Place a layer of flowers on the silica gel, making sure they are flat, then cover them with more crystals. You can dry several layers at one time. Close the lid tightly and leave them for between 18 and 24 hours, but no longer. Remove the flowers, handling them very carefully as they will be dry, although still pliable, and use a fine paintbrush to remove any grains of silica gel that adhere to the petals. Then press them in the usual way.

You will have to experiment to find the ideal time to leave the flowers in the silica gel — too long and the petals become so dry that they disintegrate in the press. If in doubt, err on the side of less time rather than more.

When they are partially dried in this way and then pressed, African violets retain their beautifully deep shades of purple and the little gold stamens seem brighter than ever. I have even successfully dried and pressed a variety that has cerise petals edged with white. I also use this technique for ordinary garden violets (which normally lose every vestige of colour in a press), and for bluebells and love-in-a-mist, which are notorious for losing their colour in the press but which, in silica gel, seem to become an even more intense shade. I am sure you will enjoy trying out this process on other difficult plants and experimenting with shorter and longer times in the crystals to suit different climates and flowers.

Autumn Colours, Damp and Pests

The yellows and reds of autumn leaves are most rewarding for the flowers presser. Strangely enough, damp and even rain do not always affect the pressing of leaves. I have even managed to press successfully a sodden mass of maple leaves that had been left, forgotten, for several days after being gathered.

Flowers, too, can be rescued from the rain, although they need rather more care. Dry them off with plenty of tissues and place them in a press in the airing cupboard. Change the blotting-paper, nappy liners, newspaper and, if used, the cardboard for at least three days running, leaving the press in a warm place for from six to eight weeks, checking it every so often for signs of damp.

Trees change colour all over the world, but I have yet to find a more useful one than stag's horn sumach

(*Rhus typhina*). Deep green at first, it changes to pale green, then yellow, then scarlet, with beautifully fringed, deeply cut leaves. All the maples are good value, as are the various creepers, some of which start off the palest pink and deepen to darkest crimson. The secret is to pick them just before they fall, and the wonderful colours will stay for ever. For strange colours and mutations in shape, it sometimes pays to look where weedkiller has been applied. Leaves sometimes turn patchily white, which can look most attractive.

Every gardener wages an ongoing battle with pests, and the flower presser is not spared. Greenfly seem to appear at every season, both outdoors and in the greenhouse, but they do have their advantages. Ordinary white lawn daisies become tinged with pink when there are greenfly lurking around. Similarly, sea carrot (*Daucus carota*) and giant hogweed (*Heracleum mantegazzianum*) turn pink when cuckoo spit is nesting in the flower-heads. Rinse the flowers under fast-running water to wash the bugs out, and then place them in a jar of water to revive and dry.

There are several strategies the

Never overlook the part that foliage of all kinds can play in your pressed flower designs. Not only will the addition of leaves and tendrils make all your arrangements look more natural and three-dimensional, but leaves have such a diversity of shape and texture that they can make the simplest of flowers look interesting. It is possible to press autumn leaves to retain their wonderful, glowing colours, and ferns can be used to give shape and form to the background of many different arrangements.

flower presser can adopt to deal with pests.

☐ Spray the plants just before they flower with a systemic insecticide. (This helps only if you remember in time!)

☐ Spray the flowers with insecticide, although this can mark them.

☐ Stand the cut flowers loosely in a jar of water next to an insecticidal strip and leave for 24 hours.

☐ If you suspect that only a few are present, gently tap the flower with your finger while holding it over a piece of white paper. You will be able to see the greenfly fall off.

Some flowers, such as candytuft (*Iberis umbellata*), are notorious for harbouring little black mites. These live, even in the press, for months, and they can be a real nuisance because their sustenance in the press consists of your carefully selected and pressed flowers. You can spray the tissues with insecticide and leave them to dry completely before using; if the infestation is bad, spray the blotting-paper, too. Alternatively, sprinkle the blotting-paper only with flea powder, but take care that no powder can reach the flowers. I have had reasonable success with both methods.

No pest will survive a burst in the microwave. After pressing material for about one week, when the flowers are quite dry and flat, place them between two pieces of blotting-paper and put them in the microwave with a cup of water on the side. Microwave on 'high' for not more than 30 seconds. Check that the flowers are not too hot every 10 seconds. This should put paid to any little pests that happen to be lurking among the petals.

2. SIMPLE PROJECTS

THE projects described in this chapter use rubber-based adhesive to create some simple but pretty items — stationery, gift tags and so forth — that are a delight to make and a joy to receive.

NOTEPAPER

Arrange a small flower design at the top left-hand side of the notepaper. Paint rubber-based adhesive mixture on the backs of the leaves and flowers and stick them down.

PLACE CARDS

Cut pieces of card 10 × 9cm (4 × 3½in). Crease the card along the centre, widthways, and fold. Open out and stick a flower and leaf on the left side, leaving room for the name in the centre and to the right.

GIFT TAGS

Cut pieces of card 7 × 5cm (2½ × 2in). Punch a hole in the top left-hand corner. Stick a small flower or design below. Thread fine ribbon or gold thread through the hole.

INVITATION CARDS

Cut pieces of card 12 × 9cm (5 × 3½in). Trim around each corner to soften the outline. Place a small arrangement of leaves and flowers in the top left-hand corner and stick as before.

You will need

- ☐ 2 small jars with lids
- ☐ adhesive cleaner
- ☐ notepaper
- ☐ rubber-based adhesive mixture (see Chapter 1)
- ☐ nylon paintbrush, no. 07
- ☐ craft knife or scalpel
- ☐ card, approximately 240gsm
- ☐ hole punch
- ☐ 3mm (1/8in) ribbon or gold thread
- ☐ fine pens, no. 01 and 02
- ☐ lighter weight, coloured card

PREVIOUS PAGE: A strong background colour can make a simple arrangement of yellows and oranges into a dramatic, eye-catching composition.

RIGHT: Fresh spring flowers have been used in this deceptively simple arrangement. Notice how foliage has been used to add interest to the flower shapes.

SMALL CARDS AND NOTELETS

A simple notelet can be made by cutting card to 17.5 × 11.5cm (7 × 4½in). Crease and fold the card widthways. Design and stick down the floral arrangement on the front. If you wish, draw a border, very lightly, 1cm (about ½in) from the edge of the card.

FINGERPLATES

It is possible to buy clear plastic fingerplates. Cut a piece of card to fit the fingerplate and arrange the plant material on the card, remembering to leave the area for the screws free. Egg white will be strong enough to hold the flowers and leaves in place.

LARGE CARDS

Cut a piece of card 45 × 20cm (18 × 8in). Measuring carefully, crease and fold it into three so that you have a card that is 20 × 15cm (8 × 6in). Open the card up and cut a window from the centre of the middle section. This can be a square, an oval, a rectangle or a circle. Draw

When you make fingerplates you can, if you wish, use coloured card or paper under the flowers to harmonize with the colour scheme of your room.

ABOVE: It is possible to buy ready-made card blanks in a range of colours and sizes, but it is easy to make your own. Use a blunt blade or the back of a knife held against a metal ruler to score the card in two places so that it folds neatly, without cracking. Use adhesive or double-sided tape to hold the right-hand flap in place.

RIGHT: When you make small cards, use single colours or shades of colours so that you do not overpower the arrangements. In the card shown at bottom right, nerines have been used to create the 'bows'.

OPPOSITE: Allow your design to break slightly out of the oval frame to soften the outline and add interest.

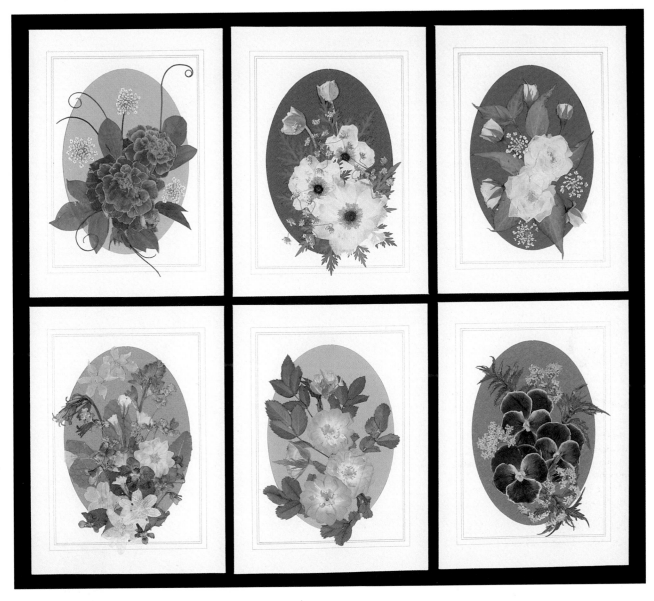

a double border about 15mm (¾in) from the edge, making sure that the outer line is a little thicker than the inner one.

Cut a piece of coloured card 15 × 10cm (6 × 4in) and glue it behind the aperture, then stick the right-hand section of the folded card to the centre section so that the back of the coloured card is enclosed and you are left with a picture frame on the front.

Arrange a design on the coloured card, letting some of the flowers and leaves slightly overlap the edge. When you are happy with the design, remove the plant material, paint adhesive solution on the back of it and stick it down.

PICTURES

All flower arrangers begin with the foliage and greenery, and so should you always start a design with the leaves. Then add any buds you are planning to include. Next, add the flowers. Stop and take a good look, re-arranging a little if necessary, tucking leaves in or over flowers to

Making a Pressed Flower Picture

After the months you have spent carefully pressing dozens of beautiful flowers and leaves comes the moment when you are ready to use your treasures. Before you begin, however, think about the background material you are going to use.

I often use velvet as I find that this gives a richness and depth not possible with paper or card. Dressmaking friends will help out with scraps of material, and your shopping expeditions will be made more interesting as you search among the remnants. Even jumble sales can produce garments that can be cut into usable pieces. Heavy silk or satin or ribbed or watered silk are good alternatives if you cannot find a particular colour in velvet. Avoid cheap, lightweight materials, which will not have the depth of colour to do justice to your flowers, and do not use bright, garish colours. Choose shades that will compliment the flowers, not detract from their natural beauty.

Pictures up to about 30cm (12in) in diameter can be mounted on fabric — silk or velvet, for example — but it is difficult to keep the material flat and taut on anything larger. Then you will have to use mounting board.

If you use paper or card, select soft greens, pinks or blues or shades of cream. Pale yellow always enhances autumnal colours. Black can be a dramatic background for white flowers, while deep green is a wonderful foil for all shades of yellow. Red is splendid for Christmas cards but not much else.

Hand-made papers have a wonderful grainy look, and they are available in some wonderful soft colours. Sugar paper, which is lighter and cheaper, can look attractive as a background, but it is not strong enough for bookmarks or greetings cards.

If you decide to use white paper, try to find a textured stock. Plain white paper has no depth to it and will always look, well, plain. You might want to try giving some good quality white paper a colour wash. Mix some watercolour paint, use a clean sponge to dampen the paper and then use another sponge or soft brush to work the colour onto the paper, trying not to leave streaks. Experiment with different colours on some spare paper — the results will be softer and subtler than commercially coloured stock. The paper may curl a little, but will soon straighten if left under some heavy books when the paint is dry.

When you are making up pressed flower pictures, remember that you cannot use a mount. The glass has to lie absolutely flat on the flowers so that the design is kept well-pressed throughout its life. Mark a border 4–6cm (1½–2½in) in from the outside edges and draw a further, finer line about 5mm (¼in) inside the outer line. This will give you the effect of a mount without the ledge.

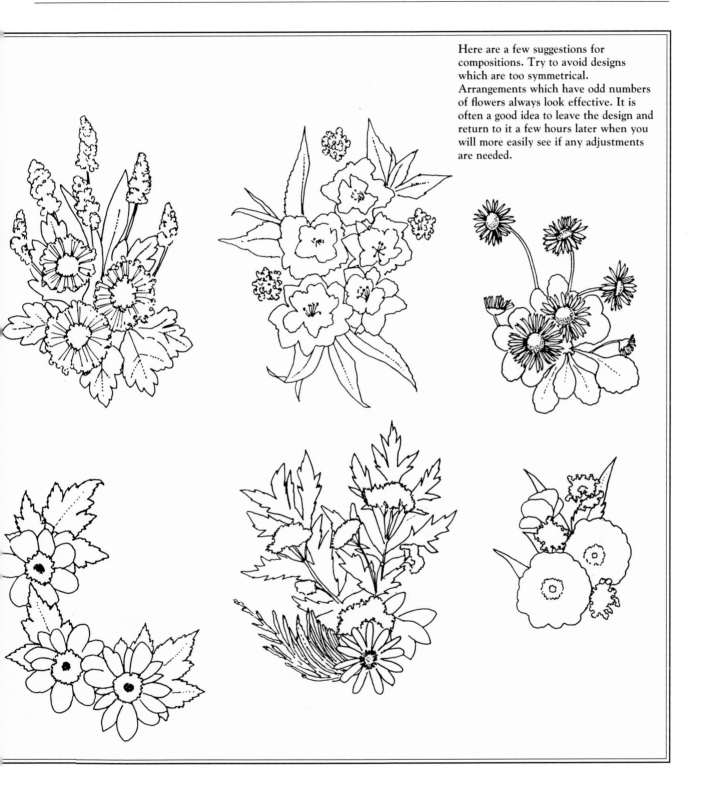

Here are a few suggestions for compositions. Try to avoid designs which are too symmetrical. Arrangements which have odd numbers of flowers always look effective. It is often a good idea to leave the design and return to it a few hours later when you will more easily see if any adjustments are needed.

Cleaning Your Brushes

Pour a small amount of adhesive cleaner into a small jar — you need only use enough to cover the bristles. Wipe off the surplus adhesive from the brush on an old tissue, then place the brush in the jar to soak for at least 15 minutes. Then, with another old tissue, squeeze off the jelly-like substance that will have formed. Replace the brush in the jar and repeat the procedure. You will probably have to do this two or three times in all.

When the brush seem quite clear of adhesive, wash it with plenty of soap and hot water, working the brush onto the soap. Rinse thoroughly and dry with a cloth or another old tissue (never throw anything away!). Good quality nylon brushes will last for years if you clean them well each time.

ABOVE: A line drawn about 1cm (½in) from the edge of a card will finish off the design neatly.

RIGHT: Suppliers of dried and pressed flower accessories have made producing pretty and useful gifts so easy — powder compacts and trinket boxes of all shapes and sizes can be transformed into presents that are a joy to receive and a delight to make.

make them look more natural. It is usually a good idea to leave the design for a few hours and then to come back to it. You will be surprised at how different it will look, and you can see more easily where to add that extra tendril or pointed leaf.

Finally — and this is the hard part — you must lift it all to one side, trying to remember where the main elements were, so that you can stick them all down with a dab of adhesive. When you are making pictures there is no need to paint adhesive on the backs of the material. Take a spatula in one hand and dip it into egg white or adhesive solution. Take the flower or leaf in a pair of tweezers, held in the other hand, and just dab it against the adhesive on the spatula. Place it on the design. This is easier than dabbing the back of the flower then picking it up. Use only the least possible amount of adhesive, so that you can easily alter the arrangement if necessary. Then leave it to dry for 24 hours before framing.

PAPERWEIGHTS AND CANDLEHOLDERS

Velvet and velour make lovely backgrounds for the clear glass paperweights and candleholders that can be
bought from dried and pressed flower
suppliers. Remember to use small,
dainty flowers and to keep your design
in proportion to the dimensions of the
item you are making.

LEFT: **Clear glass candleholders and
paperweights are available. Select a
sympathetic background material — I
like to use velvet or velour — and
simply follow the manufacturer's
instructions for placing your design in
the base.**

RIGHT AND BELOW: **When you use a
brass picture frame there is no need to
use anything stronger than beaten egg
white to hold your arrangement in
place. The glass will hold the plant
material in position. Follow the
manufacturer's instructions for
mounting your design — nothing could
be easier.**

BRASS-FRAMED PICTURES

One of the easiest ways of using
pressed flowers is to arrange them on
pieces of suitably-coloured fabric and
mount them in circular or oval brass
frames, which are available in several
sizes and which are easily dismantled
and re-assembled. You will not need
to use anything stronger than egg
white to hold the plant material in
place — the glass will keep the
arrangement in position. Trinket
boxes in a variety of shapes and sizes
are also available and can be treated
in the same way.

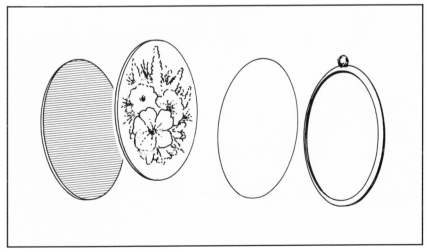

ABOVE: Daisies and buttercups can look surprisingly sophisticated against a dark background.

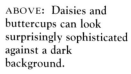

OPPOSITE: A double line around the edge of a picture gives the illusion of a mount, but in fact the design is flat against the glass. If you wish, you can use matt glass, but I prefer ordinary picture glass, which does not 'deaden' the design.

BONFIRE NIGHT PICTURE

Cut a piece of board 54 × 40cm (21 × 15½in). Wet the board with a sponge and colour wash with a blue-black mix made from indigo, cobalt and lamp black diluted in water. Mix well and test the colour. Wash the board and leave to dry, then place under heavy books for 24 hours.

Mark lines around the border with a gold pen, making the outer line heavier than the inner line.

Arrange the outside leaves to give a bonfire shape. Fill in with flame-coloured, pointed leaves to resemble fire. Tuck in some feathery grasses to resemble smoke. Place two cactus flowers, one on top of the other, to imitate fireworks.

If you need to fill in the centre of the fire, you can always use some more of the pointed cactus flowers.

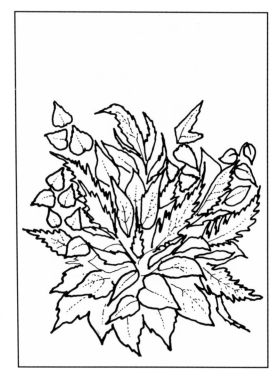

3. USING THERMASEAL

THERMASEAL should be used for all work that is in constant use, such as bookmarks, notepads, calendars and tiles. As its name suggests, it has to be heat-treated. It can be purchased in small or very large rolls, and it is perforated with tiny holes that disappear when heated. It is adhesive on one side and protected by backing paper. Simply iron it on. I prefer the gloss type. The matt finish can deaden a design, in much the same way that non-reflecting glass often seems to take all the life from a picture.

NOTEPADS

Take the front cover off the notepad and use it as a template to cut out a piece of card and a piece of Thermaseal that are 3cm (about 1½in) longer and 5mm (¼in) wider than the pad. Draw around the pad on a piece of old blotting-paper. Set out your design on the coloured card, keeping the arrangement towards the bottom.

Peel the Thermaseal off its protective backing (which you should keep for the time being) and lay it down over the blotting-paper with the adhesive side up but so that you can see the outline of the pad. Then transfer your design to the Thermaseal, working back to front. This can be rather difficult, and sometimes your arrangement will end up rather differently from how you had planned, but you will improve with practice. Then press the flowers down gently with your fingers, and place the coloured

You will need
- ☐ Thermaseal gloss film
- ☐ tweezers
- ☐ scissors
- ☐ domestic iron

If you prefer you can use coloured card or paper to match your wallpaper or furnishing. Alternatively, use the card that is supplied with the light switch cover.

card over the design. Turn it the right way up and smooth out any wrinkles.

With the iron set to medium heat and the backing paper fully covering the film, press fairly hard for about 5 seconds. Run your hand over the backing paper and lift it off. Now press the whole design down with the heel of your hand, making sure that the Thermaseal is tight against the coloured card. This can be quite hot, so you might want to use a clean, dry cloth. Leave to cool.

Place the card over the notepad, bending the top over and securing the back and top with undiluted adhesive. When it is quite firm and dry, trim all the edges flush with sharp scissors.

LIGHT SWITCH COVER

These are usually supplied with a card insert, and depending on the colour of your wall, you can use this or cut toning card to fit.

Arrange the flowers on the card, sticking them with small dabs of adhesive. Cut two pieces of Thermaseal slightly larger than the cover. Place one on top of the design and seal with an iron, using a larger piece of backing paper. Trim around the edges and remove the centre along the inner edges of the card. Place in the light switch cover. Seal with the second piece of Thermaseal on back, then trim away the centre and edges.

Ribbon bookmarks make delightful presents. There are so many different colours of ribbon available that you are sure to find one shade to match the flowers in your press.

GIFT CARDS

> **You will need**
> ☐ fine card
> ☐ fine drawing pens
> ☐ gold fingering or narrow ribbon for ties

Cut the card to 17 × 6.5cm (7 × 2¾in). Crease and fold it widthways. Draw a double or single border on the front with a fine pen about 5mm (¼in) from the edge. Cut a piece of Thermaseal to 8.5 × 6.5cm (3½ × 2¾in) so that it fits the front exactly. Arrange the flower design upside down on the Thermaseal so that it falls within the border and place it on the card. Press with a medium iron as before.

RIBBON BOOKMARKS

I have used Petersham ribbon that is 3.5cm (about 1¼in) wide, but you can use any firm, good quality cotton ribbon.

Cut the ribbon into 30cm (12in) lengths and cut the Thermaseal into pieces 30 × 8cm (12 × 3in). Draw the outline of the ribbon onto blotting-paper. Arrange the design on the ribbon. Peel off the backing paper from the Thermaseal and place it on the outline, adhesive side up. Transfer the design to the Thermaseal, working upside down and making sure that you keep within the outline. Press gently with your fingers to anchor the flowers then place the

Asparagus fern is an ideal backing for a leaf bookmark, although you can also use skelentonized leaves. Make your flower arrangements dainty and light so they do not overpower the leaves or ferns.

Skeletonizing Leaves for Bookmarks

Some shops specializing in dried flowers sell skeletonized magnolia leaves.

If you cannot obtain them in a shop and you have a friend with a magnolia tree, search among the fallen leaves in the autumn and you may find some skeletonized ones. These will need to be dried out in a warm place, then scrubbed gently but firmly to loosen any patches of old skin.

Failing this, there is a much more laborious method. Place a handful of soda crystals in a large saucepan of water. Bring this to the boil and submerge the leaves. Boil for at least 1 hour. Take out a leaf with tongs and run it under cold water. Scrape it with a brush. If the skin comes away easily, leave the other leaves in the water to cool. If it does not, boil for a little longer.

Place the leaves one by one on a firm surface and scrub to remove the loose skin. Leave to dry well before using.

ribbon over the design. Turn the Thermaseal edges over so that they meet in the centre back of the ribbon. Check that the design is in place. If it is not, open up one side and push the flowers or leaves back into position. Press well with your hand. Place the bookmark between two sheets of backing paper and finish both sides as for the notepad. Leave to cool, when it will be quite stiff. Trim the top of the bookmark with pinking shears and cut the base to a point with sharp scissors.

SMALL RIBBON BOOKMARKS

This time use ribbon that is 2.5cm (1in) wide, and cut it into 25cm (10in) lengths. Cut the Thermaseal into pieces 25 × 6cm (10 × 2¼in) and proceed as above.

LEAF BOOKMARKS

You will need skeletonized leaves or sprays of asparagus fern, approximately 18cm (7in) long and 10cm (4in) across at the widest part. Draw a rough outline of the leaf on blotting-paper and cut two pieces of Thermoseal at least 2cm (¾in) wider and longer than the leaf.

Arrange the design of flowers on the leaf. Place one piece of Thermaseal on the outline, adhesive side up. Place the flowers upside down on the Thermaseal, followed by the leaf or spray. Press fairly hard with your hand, then place the second piece of Thermaseal over the design, starting at one end and gently lowering it, making sure it does not wrinkle.

Place the whole between two large pieces of backing paper and press with a medium iron on both sides. Peel off the paper and press down well with your hand. Leave to cool and stiffen, then trim into the shape of a leaf, with natural-looking, undulating edges, tapering to a stalk at the base.

LAMPSHADES

You can either use a ready-made shade or buy a frame and cover it yourself.

If you have a plain drum or straight Empire-style shade, carefully dismantle it and lay the shade material out flat. Cut a piece of Thermaseal that is 2cm (¾in) larger all round than the material. Arrange the design of flowers and leaves, remembering that the design will have to meet at the join. Stick each item down with a spot of adhesive solution. Lower the Thermaseal down onto the shade very carefully, smoothing out any wrinkles

as you go. If you have a very large shade you will find it easier if you peel off the backing paper from the centre of the design and work outwards.

Place a large piece of backing paper over the shade material and press with a medium iron. Peel off the paper and press hard all over with your hand or a clean, dry cloth. Trim the Thermaseal to size and re-assemble the shade.

Alternatively, if you do not have a plain, ready-made lampshade that you can decorate, you can easily make one from a straight-sided frame.

You will need
- ☐ straight-sided Empire frame
- ☐ white tape
- ☐ all-purpose adhesive
- ☐ stiff card
- ☐ polyester silk
- ☐ velvet ribbon

Wind each strut of the frame with the tape and fasten it securely with a tiny dab of glue. Repeat on the top and base rings.

Cut a template from stiff card that is 2cm (¾in) wider and deeper than a

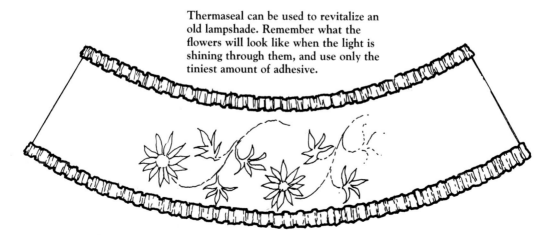

Thermaseal can be used to revitalize an old lampshade. Remember what the flowers will look like when the light is shining through them, and use only the tiniest amount of adhesive.

panel of the frame and use it to cut out six panels from the silk. Cut three Thermaseal shapes that are 2cm (¾in) shorter and narrower than the template — i.e., they should be exactly the size of the panels in the frame.

Arrange a flower design on the silk panels. When you are satisfied, place them upside down on the Thermaseal and iron on the silk, remembering to use a piece of backing paper. Make sure that they are completely sealed, especially around the edges.

Pin the panels to the struts. You will find this easier to do if you sew one panel in position before proceeding to the next. Use tiny stitches and trim the excess fabric as close to your stitch line as you dare.

Stick toning velvet ribbon onto the struts to hide the stitching and around the top and bottom rings to finish.

The simpler the shape of the lampshade
the better. Avoid shades that have
curved panels because it is more
difficult to attach the Thermaseal.

4. IDEAS FOR CHRISTMAS

MANY imperfect flowers and leaves can be sprayed with gold paint. Remember, in this instance, it is the shape you are looking for, not the colour. The paint will tend to fill in bulky flowers. A geum, for example, will look too solid, whereas the spiky edges and pronounced stamens of astrantia are perfect. Old bluebells and the deeply fringed leaves of stag's horn sumach will look wonderfully dramatic.

Red, green, deep blue or even black card is suitable, or you could use gold flowers on a cream-coloured background for a golden wedding card.

CHRISTMAS CARDS

To make the Christmas tree cards use bright red or green card and cut a piece 30 × 20cm (12 × 8in). Score and fold it widthways. Draw two border lines with a fine gold pen about 2cm (¾in) from the edges.

Choose a fern that most resembles a Christmas tree; the buckler ferns (*Dryopteris*) are the best.

Use a rubber-based adhesive to fix the fern to the centre of the card. Make a 'tub' by cutting a large leaf into shape; deep maroon ivy leaves or the petals from a snake's head fritillary will do for this.

Place a cow parsley flower as a star at the top of the tree, then stick 7–9 marguerite petals on the 'branches', placing them upside down so that the bases of the petals resemble the wicks of the candles.

Now you can have some fun adding the decorations. Tiny petals, single

Most people think of summer when they think of pressed flower arrangements. However, you can make a wonderful array of Christmas decorations with some brightly coloured card and a tin of gold spray paint. When you come to make cards and table decorations for Christmas, you can use some of the less successful items from your press. As long as the flowers or leaves are a pleasing shape, a blemish or two will be unnoticeable when they have been sprayed with gold.

OPPOSITE: **Use this template to cut out pieces of green or red card. You can increase or decrease the size by enlarging or reducing the size of the grid squares. Use short lengths of gold fingering to hang the finished decorations from your Christmas tree.**

forget-me-not flowers, rape flowers, coral bells, minute sprays of yellow alyssum — use whatever you have that is tiny and bright, but don't use too many or you will swamp the tree.

'The Three Wise Men' cards can also be made from bright red or green card, but a deep blue will look very effective. Cut a piece 30 × 20cm (12 × 8in), score it and fold it widthways.

Arrange conifer leaves along the base and half-way up the sides. Place three *Dicentra alba* 'men' in the foreground, giving them 'bouquets' to hold and 'hats' of tiny pink chervil flowers. Make a star in the top right-hand corner from three chincherinchee flowers, one on top of the other. A simple, but dramatic design.

Other simple, but striking designs can be made by using gold-sprayed foliage and flowers on dark backgrounds. (See below.)

SMALL CARDS

Cut some white card to 18 × 12cm (7 × 5in). Score and fold it lengthways. Use adhesive solution to stick a red cactus flower (Easter cactus, *Rhipsalidopsis*) in the centre. Stick two more over the top, making sure that the petals point in all directions. Place the stamens from a celandine or buttercup in the centre.

CHRISTMAS GIFT TAGS

You can make two tags at the same time. Place fern leaves about 10cm (4in) apart on a sheet of red, green or white card. Anchor each one down with a fine dress-making pin. Make sure you cover your table or working surface with newspaper and spray the whole sheet of card gold, sweeping the spray can across and up and down to obtain good coverage. Lift off the ferns after a minute or two and leave them to dry. The gold-sprayed card

will have the silhouettes of the ferns, and these can be cut to the required shape. Punch a hole in the top left-hand corner and thread through some ribbon or thread. The gold ferns can then be stuck on some contrasting card, which can be cut into gift tags as before.

CHRISTMAS PLACE CARDS

Cut pieces of red or green card to 10 × 9cm (4 × 3½in). Score the card and fold it widthways. With a fine gold pen, draw a border measuring 3 × 3.5cm (1¼ × 1½in) on the left hand-side of the card and fix a gold-sprayed leaf or flower in this box. Write the guest's name in gold on the right.

CHRISTMAS DECORATIONS

You will need
- □ stiff red or green card
- □ compass or plate with a smooth, round edge
- □ ruler
- □ adhesive
- □ gold-sprayed flowers and leaves
- □ gold thread for hanging

Start with a circle about 16cm (6½in) in diameter and divide it into eight equal sections. I am no mathematician and I usually guess — you can always trim off the odd bits later on. Draw a line across the base of each section. Cut out two adjoining sections. Score and fold on the lines. Open them out and stick the gold flowers and/or leaves on five of the

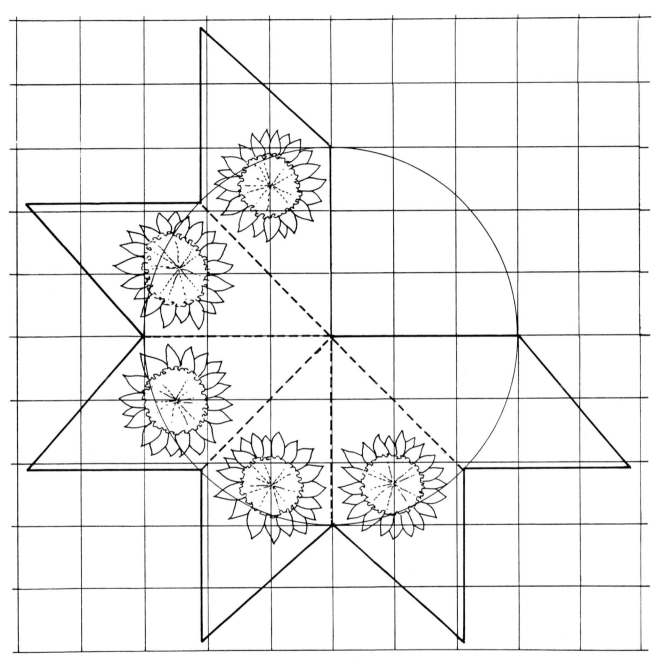

sections, then bend them around, gluing the blank section under one of the flowered sections. Cut a tiny hole in the top and make a loop of gold thread, knotting it inside so that it can be hung up.

You can draw scallops around the base of each section, using either a compass or the lid of a small jar before proceeding as above.

To make pointed decorations, draw a circle 12cm (about 5in) in diameter

and draw equal points about 4cm (1½in) from the base of each section before proceeding as above.

You can make smaller decorations for the Christmas tree by decreasing the size of the circle.

5. PROJECTS FOR SPECIAL OCCASIONS

Wedding Pictures

IT CAN BE both a delight and a trial to make a picture from a bride's bouquet. Quite often one is presented with a rather bedraggled bouquet, at least two days old and probably going brown at the edges. If you are asked to design a picture *before* the big day, it is a good idea to suggest that you have a selection of the flowers before they are all wired up for the bouquet — but that is the ideal.

You can at least recommend that the bouquet is kept as dry as possible and stored in a cool place. Also that you should receive it, at the latest, the day after the ceremony.

Before you dismantle the arrangement, make a brief sketch of the shape of the bouquet, noting the positions of the principle flowers and leaves, so that when the bride sees the picture she is reminded of the happiest of days. Even better, of course, would be a colour photograph.

An oval frame always seems to be more romantic and appropriate for a wedding picture, especially if it is painted with antique gold paint. Perhaps, too, you could use some of the material of the wedding dress or from the bridesmaids' dresses for the background.

Carefully take the bouquet to pieces, separating each flower or spray, if they are not too thick, and any foliage that can be used. Press whole flowers if you can, because they will give depth to the picture. Carnations press amazingly successfully if

LEFT: It can be both a privilege and a problem to be asked to make up a bridal bouquet into a picture. Your aim must always be to try to reproduce the overall shape and colours of the original even though the finished picture will, inevitably, be much smaller.

you cut off only a small part of the calyx. Be careful, though. If you cut off too much the petals will fall out. Press the calyx and petals of buds separately. Rosebuds should be cut in half. Small, whole roses can be pressed easily, but anything too large or thick should be taken apart and the petals pressed separately. Poppy or anemone stamens make good make-believe centres for roses. Freesias should be divided into two or three and pressed flat. Freesia buds can be pressed as a spray.

Do not try to press any sort of lily. They are notorious for ending up a slimy brown mess! Freesias make a very good substitute.

Discard any flowers that have brown edges. If all the white flowers are fading, you can trim a few and even, as a last resort, touch up the backs of some petals with very thin, creamy white acrylic paint after they have been pressed for two or three weeks.

Little bits and pieces such as ribbons and lace and even confetti can be popped into the press and used, with great restraint, in the final picture.

Change the blotting-paper, nappy liners and newspaper after two days to make sure that the flowers dry quickly. Then leave for eight weeks.

Most wedding pictures are smaller than the original bouquet, and sometimes a little judicious cheating is in order. You may have some smaller, appropriately coloured roses already in your press, or you may have some pressed lily-of-the-valley sprays, which can take the place of some small lilies. Instead of using agapanthus, which does not, in any case, take kindly to pressing, you could use blue lace flower (*Didiscus caeruleus* syn. *Trachymene caerulea*) and tuck

this in behind some other flowers to produce just the right flash of blue.

When you come to arrange the picture, use your sketch or photograph as a guide. Start with the outline shape of the bouquet, using leaves or ferns and making a fairly solid background, especially if the fabric behind is white or cream. Build up the design with larger flowers. Place some of the leaves or ferns over and around the flowers, and tuck in the odd bud to give a natural look.

Although the whole design is smaller than the original bouquet, try to recreate the shape and colours as closely as possible. Sometimes an odd leaf or flowers from another source has to be added to give the picture depth and balance, but remember that it is the bride's flowers and hers alone that will bring back the memories.

Valentine Card

You will need
- [ ] double-fold card, 20 × 15cm (8 × 6in) with a pre-cut, heart-shaped aperture about 10 x 10cm (4 × 4in)
- [ ] polyester silk, 15 × 13cm (6 × 5in)
- [ ] Thermaseal, 15 × 13cm (6 × 5in)
- [ ] rubber-based adhesive
- [ ] wadding, 10 × 9cm (4 × 3½in)
- [ ] lace, 65cm (24in)
- [ ] ribbon to tone with flower design, 20cm (8in)

Using the card as a guide, draw an outline of the heart on a piece of paper. Place Thermaseal, adhesive side up, over the outline and arrange the design on it, upside down. Place silk over the Thermaseal, press down well, turn over and iron on, remembering to use a backing sheet.

Put a spot of adhesive in each corner and stick the design under the aperture, making sure it is in the centre and well within the borders of the heart.

Stick the wadding over the back with a dot of adhesive in each corner, then smear adhesive all around the edges of the right-hand page of the card and stick it to the centre panel to enclose the design.

Run a gathering thread through the lace and draw it up to 33cm (13in). Smear a thin line of adhesive around the heart and stick the lace in place, with the ends just turned in and meeting at the base of the heart. Make a small bow of ribbon and glue it over the join.

LAVENDER BAGS

You will need
☐ polyester silk or similar fabric
☐ 3cm (1¼in) wide lace
☐ Thermaseal
☐ narrow ribbon
☐ lavender flowers or pot pourri
☐ small kitchen funnel

Cut two rectangles of silk, each measuring 18 × 14cm (7 x 5½in), and cut one rectangle of Thermoseal, measuring 15 x 11cm (6 × 4½in). Arrange a flower design on one piece of silk and transfer it, upside down, to

the adhesive side of the Thermaseal. Place it on the silk exactly 1.5cm (½in) from the edge all round. Using a large piece of backing paper to cover the silk, press with a medium iron for only 5 seconds. Remove the paper and press hard with your hand. If it is not completely sealed, especially around the edges, repeat the process.

Pin the two pieces of silk together with the wrong sides facing. Run a gathering thread through the edge of the lace and pin it 1.5cm (½in) from the outside edges. The edge of the lace will be right up to the edge of the Thermaseal on the top panel. Ease the fullness of the lace around the corners. Pin a loop of ribbon to tone with the flowers between the silk at the top.

Sew through the lace, the silk and, when you reach it, the ribbon with tiny herring-bone stitches, leaving a

ABOVE: I prefer to leave a fabric border of about 1cm (less than ½in) behind the lace. Trim it carefully with pinking shears to stop the fabric from fraying.

OPPOSITE: What could be more romantic than a specially made, heart-shaped card? White cotton lace can be coloured a delicate shade of cream by dipping it in black coffee.

gap at the bottom. Fill the bag through this hole, using the funnel. Complete the sewing. Turn the bag over and trim the seams with pinking shears, leaving 1cm (a bit less than ½in) all round. Trim the corners across. You can use a machine to stitch around the edge, but a hand-sewn bag always seems to make a more personal gift.

These bags can be given as a gift on their own or they can be used to form the front of a card, with a suitable message inside. Store the scented bags in sealed plastic bags to retain their scent.

DECORATING GLASS

> **You will need**
> ☐ clean glass container
> ☐ tin of automotive clear lacquer

You must work in a very well venti-lated room, if not outdoors, when you use this laquer.

Spray the jar with laquer and fix a design of flowers and leaves around the lower centre of the jar, remember-ing that the design must meet. Alter-natively, paint the backs of the leaves and flowers with undiluted rubber-based glue to stick them to the glass. Leave to dry for 20–30 minutes, then give it three or four finishing coats, allowing at least 20 minutes between each coat. The flowers should be completely sealed. For extra durability you can paint a thin coat of resin over the jar, taking care to remove any drips before they dry hard. Leave for 24 hours.

This method can be successfully used on any hard surface, including enamel and wood. Most craft shops stock blank wooden items, which you can decorate, and a perfectly plain, inexpensive enamel mug can be trans-formed by the addition of a flower design. Kitchen shops are a great source of inspiration!

Some flowers change colour or darken in the process, so you must experiment, making use of shapes to enhance your designs.

RIGHT: The range of items that can be decorated with pressed flowers and leaves under coats of protective lacquer is virtually limitless. Look around craft and gift shops for plain wooden kitchen ware, which can be transformed into unusual and attractive gifts.

CANDLES

You will need
- [ ] night light
- [ ] flowerpot
- [ ] used, white candle wax
- [ ] empty baby food tin
- [ ] aluminium foil
- [ ] paintbrush, size 07 or 08
- [ ] candles, any size but preferably white

Place the night light under the flowerpot (you could use a perfume oil burner instead). Put clean, used white candle wax in the tin and place it over the night light to melt. It is a good idea to set the whole thing on a sheet of aluminium foil for safety.

When the wax is melted and hot, place a leaf or flower on the candle, holding it with one hand. Dip the brush in the hot wax and paint over the leaf. Repeat around the candle, adding flowers and leaves as you wish. Keep the brush in the wax as much as possible to prevent it from hardening and becoming unworkable.

ABOVE: Candles decorated with pressed flowers are almost too pretty to light! Plain white candles can be made to look quite exceptional, and the technique is surprisingly simple.

OPPOSITE: Ceramic tiles decorated with pressed flowers and coated in Thermaseal will withstand hot casserole dishes, and they are ideal teapot mats. Wipe clean with a damp cloth.

TILE COASTERS AND PLACE MATS

You will need

☐ For large mats: 15cm (6in) square ceramic tile; 19cm (7½in) square Thermaseal; 14.5cm (5¾in) square fablon velour backing

☐ For small mats: 11cm (4½in) square ceramic tile; 15cm (6in) square Thermaseal; 10.25cm (4¼in) square fablon velour backing

Whichever size tile you are using, make an outline on blotting-paper. Collect the flowers and leaves you have decided to use before you start and arrange the design on the tile. Peel the Thermaseal off the backing paper and lay it on the outline, adhesive side up. Transfer the design upside down to the Thermaseal. Lightly press the design with your fingers. Carefully turn over and place the Thermaseal on the tile. If any flowers slip in the process, lift up the Thermaseal and push them back into place. Press out any wrinkles.

Turn over and fold the opposite edges of the Thermaseal onto the tile. Clip the corners and fold over the other sides. Pre-heat the oven to 140°C (280°F). Place the tile on a heat-resistant, up-turned bowl, making sure that the Thermaseal does not touch any surface, and leave in the oven for about 1½ minutes. Remove from the oven and press down all over the with heel of your hand, including the back and the sides of the tile. It will not be too hot.

When completely cold, finish the back by applying fablon velour to cover the edges of the Thermaseal.

These tiles will stand quite hot casserole dishes, teapots and mugs, and they make excellent table mats.

FLORAL CLOCK

You will need

☐ coloured card or thick paper, colour washed

☐ plate or compass

☐ quartz clock movement and pair of hands

☐ Thermaseal

☐ frame

Cut the card or paper to 31 × 28cm (12½ × 11in). Colour wash it if you are using paper (see Chapter 2). Mark a circle with a faint line around a plate or with a compass so that it is 23cm (9in) in diameter.

Cover the pencil line with florets of cow parsley. Arrange different flowers at the hour stations. Place the stalks of *Alchemilla alpina* in between each set of flowers and the leaves, with their pretty, silky silver backs upwards, to cover the stalks.

Cut a hole in the centre, and arrange white candytuft flowers around it. Cut the Thermaseal slightly larger than the card and gently lower it on to the design. Heat seal. Frame with the backboard and attach the clock mechanism.

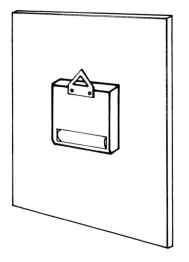

ABOVE AND RIGHT: Quartz clock movements are available in several styles, but they are all easy to fit. Choose a style of hands that will suit the flowers you want to use.

WALL HANGING

You will need

- [ ] coarse material (such as linen or curtain lining) cut to 65 × 28cm (26 x 11in)
- [ ] mounting board, 60 × 11.5cm (24 × 4½in)
- [ ] one pair of wooden bell-pull dowel rods and end pieces, 12cm (5in) wide
- [ ] rubber-based adhesive, diluted with water
- [ ] thread to match material

Fold the material lengthwise, inside out, and sew the seam 2cm (¾in) from the edge. Turn the material to the right side and press the seam flat, making sure it runs down the centre back.

Turn under the top and bottom edges by 5mm (¼in). Turn 3cm (1¼in) over at the top towards the back and pin, just through the back thickness. Slip the mounting board inside and pin the bottom as for the top. Hem the turning, leaving about 2cm (¾in) open at each side. Slip the dowel rods into place and glue the ends.

Arrange the design on the front. When you are satisfied paint the backs of the flowers and foliage with diluted adhesive and replace them on the fabric, making sure they are thoroughly attached. Dip a cocktail stick into the adhesive if any leaf ends or errant petals need attention so that you can add just a spot of glue. Press them down.

You can cover wall hangings with Thermaseal, but I think they look more natural without.

Tendrils and dainty leaves are ideal for long, thin arrangements.

6. WORKING WITH RESIN

I MUST ADMIT that I approached working with resin with some trepidation. However, as with all modern materials, it really is quite easy. There are, nevertheless, one or two ground rules to observe for safety's sake:

☐ Adults must supervise any children who use resin.

☐ Always work in a well-ventilated room. The 27°C (80°F) recommended by the manufacturer is almost impossible to achieve in a normal home with all the windows open. My thermometer registered 18°C (65°F) and everything seemed perfectly satisfactory.

☐ Use barrier cream on your hands or wear fine, hairdresser's gloves.

☐ If possible, wear a mask and safety spectacles.

☐ Have everything you need ready before you begin.

☐ Never smoke or use naked flame.

Resin is surprisingly easy to use, and it protects the colours of the flower material beneath it. You will use all your stocks of tiny, delicate flowers and leaves when you begin to make jewellery.

You will need

- ☐ proprietary, two-part epoxy, which is supplied in two containers

- ☐ hypodermic syringes; for small work, such as jewellery, 10ml is sufficient

- ☐ polypropylene cups, size depending on the items to be decorated

- ☐ mixing sticks; the sticks used in lollipops are ideal or buy sticks from a craft supplier

- ☐ wooden cocktail sticks for small items

- ☐ coloured pastes; several shades are available, which can be mixed to create subtle shades (buy larger jars of white to use as a base colour)

- ☐ low-tack, double-sided tape, which you will use to anchor items to be filled with resin to keep them steady

- ☐ flat piece of board, about 10 × 5cm (4 × 2in); when you work on items such as rings and brooches you will need a larger piece of wood with grooves cut into it

- ☐ large piece of aluminium foil to protect your working surface

- ☐ dress-making pins for pricking bubbles, which may rise to the surface

- ☐ acetone for cleaning

- ☐ paintbrushes, no. 06 or 07

EARRINGS

You will have enough resin for 12 pairs of earrings. Cover a flat working surface with aluminium foil. Place the flat piece of board in front of you and cut tiny pieces of low-tack tape to attach to the back of the earrings. Remove the back of the tape and stick the earrings to the board so that they remain flat and steady while you work.

Mix the resin. Use a hypodermic syringe to draw off 5ml from each bottle and place them in a mixing cup. Use a stick to stir gently but very thoroughly for about 2 minutes. Using a cocktail stick, add a little white paste. Mix gently, adding more white paste until the resin mix is completely white.

Using the same cocktail stick, apply a thin layer of white mix to the base of six earrings, making sure it completely covers the area, right up to the edges.

Then, with another cocktail stick, add a tiny drop of red paste to the white base, and stir gently to create a pale pink. Cover the base of six earrings as above. You can now add a drop of blue paste, which should mix to a harebell blue or, if you have been too enthusiastic, a pale mauve shade. Use this on another six earrings. Finally, add a good drop of black paste, stirring well and adding more until you have a deep black. Cover the base of the remaining six earrings. Arrange your designs on the coloured resins and make sure that they are well anchored. Because they are tiny, earrings will take all your smallest flowers — forget-me-nots, London pride, candytuft florets, ferns, pink chervil, tiny pansies and yellow alyssum, perhaps. Some flowers lose their colours in this process, but can produce attractive results. I used blue lace flower on a pink background and some of the flowers turned to lime

green, which gave an unusual and rather pleasing effect. Leave to dry for 24 hours or so

Throw away the sticks. Clean the cup and syringes with old tissues and wipe with tissue dipped in acetone.

Mix the two resins together as before, stirring them well for 2 minutes but leaving them clear this time. Twirl a cocktail stick in the mixture and let a large drop fall in the centre of the design. Push the resin carefully towards the edges. You may have to add another drop to cover the base of the earring completely. Complete all the earrings in the same way. If any bubbles rise to the surface of the clear resin, prick them with a small pin or blow gently on them. Place them in an airing cupboard for 24 hours, making sure that they stay dust-free by covering with a tray or a box.

Keep them in a warm place for at least a week before adding the ear wires or studs.

BROOCHES AND RINGS

These larger items are treated in exactly the same way as the earrings except, of course, you will need more resin, and you can use a paintbrush to spread it.

You will also need a larger board with grooves cut in it in which you can balance the bulky backs. Everything must lie absolutely flat or the resin will run to one side or corner.

Resin stays workable for only about 20 minutes, so it is best to mix just enough for a few items at a time. If you are using several colours you

ABOVE: When you make brooches or rings you will need a board with a groove cut in it so that you can hold the items perfectly flat while you work on them. If you do not do this, the resin will run to one side.

RIGHT: Decorate white porcelain with plant material under resin. The flowers will not fade in sunlight.

should mix one, use it, then mix another and use that, unless you have enough time and resin to mix and shade as described for the earrings.

DECORATING PORCELAIN

Work out your design on the plates or bowls before you prepare the resin mix. When you are quite happy, mix the resin in fairly small quantities — not more than 10ml of each. Pour a little onto the plate and use a paintbrush to spread it right out to the sides in a sweeping movement until it is evenly distributed. Place the first layer of leaves or flowers on the sticky surface. If any pieces of plant material overlap, brush a little resin underneath to help them stick. Leave for a few hours in a warm place.

Place a flower on the shiny side of Thermaseal backing paper and hold it down with a cocktail stick. Use a paintbrush to brush it all over the underside with resin. Quickly lift it with tweezers onto the plate and into position. Repeat with the other elements of your design. Alternatively, brush a layer of resin over the whole design area and place the next

You could thread narrow coloured ribbon through the pierced edge of the porcelain to finish off your design if you wish.

layer of flowers and leaves on to it, repeating this until you have built up the whole design and leaving each layer to dry between coats.

Finish with a layer of resin, brushing the sides slightly towards the centre to prevent a hard edge from forming. Cover the items with a tray or box to exclude dust and leave in a warm place for 24 hours. Store in a warm, dry place for a week.

Every time you use resin, some little air bubbles will rise to the surface. If these are very obvious, you can prick them with a pin or blow on them fairly hard to achieve a smooth surface.

RESIN AND PICTURES

Most floral material will fade over time, particularly the foliage. The greener it is, the more it will fade, especially if it is placed in strong light. However, many items can be coated with a thin layer of resin, which will keep, and even enhance, their colours.

You will need

☐ non-stick paper (the shiny side of Thermaseal backing paper is ideal)

☐ two-part epoxy resin

☐ measuring cup

☐ mixing and cocktail sticks

☐ tweezers

☐ paintbrush, no. 07

☐ acetone for cleaning

Assemble your design so that you know roughly how the picture will look when it is completed. Mix 10ml of each part of the resin.

Taking each flower, leaf or spray separately, place it on non-stick paper. Hold it down with a mixing stick or cocktail stick, paint a thin coat of resin all over the front. Remove to a clean piece of non-stick paper and leave to dry for 24 hours in a warm dry place.

Take great care with the material, which will be quite brittle. Use the pieces to build up pictures as you wish — they will never fade, even in bright sunlight.

You can also use plant material that has been treated in this way to decorate items that will be left in daylight — coat hooks, for example — and that might otherwise fade or be damaged by daily use.

★ ★ ★

Cleaning your tools and utensils is quite simple if you use acetone, which is available from most craft suppliers. Still wearing your rubber gloves, wipe out the mixing cup with an old tissue, pour a little acetone into it and swirl the paintbrush, wiping it with an old tissue.

Take the hypodermic syringe apart, dip it in the acetone and wipe it.

Remember to wipe your tweezers, too.

There will still be a little acetone left in the cup, so wipe that out with tissue and clean any drips on the outside.

Rub your protective gloves with the impregnated tissue to remove any resin. Still wearing your gloves, wash everything in hot, soapy water. Rinse and dry.

Always make sure your room is well-ventilated because acetone is very potent — open all your windows as far as you can.

THE
PRESSED FLOWER
GARDEN

THE PRESSED FLOWER GARDEN

EVERYONE will have their own favourite plants in their garden and in the countryside, but I have listed here some of the plants that I enjoy growing in my garden and that I have used in the projects illustrated in this book.

Annuals

If some other flowers are the stars, then the annuals can justly be described as the chorus line. They give the flower presser all the colours of the rainbow to explore, and they are easy to grow, thriving on being picked and providing more and more blooms to delight the eye. When you have enough for your purposes, they seem to give a collective sigh of relief and reward you with an extra burst of exuberance.

Acroclinium roseum (Helipterum roseum)
Pink or white daisy-like, straw-textured flowers, which keep their colour well.

Ammi major Queen Anne's lace, Cow parsley
A superior form, with larger, whiter umbels and florets.

Brachycome iberidifolia Swan River daisy
Daisy-like flowers, usually deep purple with yellow centres. They press well but curl up when removed from the press, so you have to work fast. The petals are inclined to lose colour.

Calendula officinalis Pot marigold
The ordinary garden pot marigold develops a magnificent shot silk look when pressed. Choose all the shades, particularly those with dark centres.

Press buds at all stages of development. Good, lasting colour.

Centaurea cyanus Cornflower, Bluebottle
Pull out the petals and press them separately. They are like little blue fans with pointed edges.

Chrysanthemum frutescens (Argyranthemum frutescens) Marguerite
Wonderful pristine white petals and bright yellow centres if they are picked early enough. Otherwise, they fall to pieces after pressing. Use petals as 'candles' on Christmas trees.

Consolida ambigua (C. ajacis, Delphinium consolida) Larkspur
A very rewarding flower, as it never seems to lose its colour. A mixed packet of seed will give blue, pink and white flowers — and all shades in between. Press single flowers and the sprays of buds. The dwarf Hyacinth-flowered series has spikes of smaller flowers.

Cosmos Cosmos Bright Lights series
The bright orange, yellow or scarlet flowers can be pressed whole, in spite of the rather pronounced centre. The red petals turn a deep mahogany colour. Only the dark pinks press well. Press lots of buds and leaves, which can be used in many designs.

Cynoglossum nervosum Chinese forget-me-not, Himalayan hound's tongue
Intensely blue flowers, rather like large forget-me-nots. Pick sprays, removing most of the unopened buds.

Didiscus caeruleus (Trachymene caerulea) Blue lace flower
Like small, open scabious. Pale blue when grown in a greenhouse, but a deeper shade outdoors.

Gypsophila elegans Gypsophila
This annual species has small white, single flowers. Press singly or in sprays.

Iberis umbellata Candytuft
Surely one of the flower presser's favourite flowers. Cut the heads just below the lowest open floret.

Lathyrus odoratus Sweet pea
Press only the dark shades because the others fade easily, although the white becomes a good cream colour. Press heads after removing some flowers. They take ages to dry.

Layia platyglossa (L. elegans) Tidy tips
A little known annual, but well worth growing. Has white-tipped, gold-petalled, daisy-like flowers, with dramatic black and gold centres.

Limnanthes douglasii Poached-egg flower, Meadow foam
As the common name suggests, these 2.5cm (1in) wide flowers are white

with deep gold centres. They flower profusely and seed themselves. The petals are delicate, so handle them with care. The deeply cut leaves are also useful.

Lobelia erinus
The trailing varieties are easiest to pick. Find dark and pale blue varieties that have white eyes. Press individual flowers and sprays, taking care to dab off the milky juice that exudes from the stalks before pressing.

Lunaria annua Honesty
Press the violet or white flowers as sprays; later press the tiny green seed pods; finally, remove the outer husk and press the pearly white pods. Scatter a few seeds in the autumn every year.

Lupinus Lupin
Most shades are disappointing, but the deep blue-and-white bi-colour stays reasonably true in the press. Pick individual florets and use them to make butterflies.

Malcolmia maritima Virginian stock
Very good value if you press whole sprays of the deeper shades.

Myosotis Forget-me-not
Remove any leaves that overlap the flowers. Press whole sprays and individual florets.

Nemophila menziesii (*N. insignis*)
Baby blue-eyes
The sky blue flowers with white centres have delicate petals, which can fade. Use 2–3 flowers to give depth.

Papaver burseri (*P. alpinum*)
Alpine poppy
These are good self-seeders and the only poppy worth pressing. Choose the brighter colours as they do fade a little. Remove the hard centre with a twist, retaining the stamens. When you are using them, place 2–3 on top of each other to give depth.

Salpiglossis sinuata Salpiglossis Bolero series
Velvety, heavily veined petals make funnel-shaped flowers. These can be slit down one side and pressed open to make an instant fan. Use all colours.

Salvia farinacea 'Victoria'
Dark blue flower-filled spikes should be picked with the distinctive blue stalks. Some white varieties, which have a white stalk, are available. They all lend height to a design.

Salvia horminium Clary
Bright pink, purple and white bracts can be pressed as a spray or singly. The white can sometimes turn a disappointing brown.

Scabiosa Scabious
Lavender blue cushion-like flowers with a dense central disc. The darker varieties are best.

Schizanthus Butterfly flower,
Poor man's orchid
Try to make sure the attractive markings are displayed when you press the flowers.

Tagetes patula French marigold
Choose a variety that has double flowers of all shades, some with contrasting edges to the petals. Pick the flowers only in dry weather and press whole, cutting off a very small part of the calyx. Although they seem bulky, they press well. Change the paper and keep in the press for at least 8 weeks.

Ursina anthemoides
A bright orange, daisy-like flower with deep mahogany centres. They must be picked in the sun as they are inclined to close in dull weather.

Verbena
Press the florets separately, using the deep colours, some of which have dark eyes.

Xeranthemum Immortelles
An everlasting flower that presses beautifully. The paler colours have a sheen on them, and they can look like water-lilies when they are placed on a dark background.

Perennials and Biennials
These are the reliable stars of the show, giving you flowers and foliage year after year. Just a little feeding and a good mulch to stop them drying out, and they are yours for the taking. All plants benefit from dead-heading — and this is, after all, what you are doing, only a little earlier. Bear this in mind when you are cutting for the press and they will never disappoint you.

Achillea millefolium 'Rose Queen'
Divide the flat heads in small sprays. Also press the small single florets. Do not be put off by the hard calyx.

Alchemilla mollis Lady's mantle
Press these yellow, intricately branched heads of flowers when they are fully out. The leaves have rounded, serrated edges and must be picked only when very dry because they gather water.

Anchusa azurea (*A. italica*)
The deep gentian blue flowers are similar to forget-me-nots, and they should be picked as sprays. Remove some leaves and buds.

Anemone blanda
All varieties keep their colour well and the rarer white blooms are especially useful — catch them before the slugs do!

Anemone × *fulgens*
The large, brightly coloured blooms with black centres are useful in large, dramatic pictures.

Anemone × *hybrida* (*A. japonica*)
The pink and white flowers press and keep their colour well. The double pink varieties are almost prettier seen from the back, which seems shot with silver silk. Use another centre to complete the flower.

Aquilegia Columbine,
Granny's bonnets
Although they look awkward to press, they can be pressed successfully. The large, bright garden varieties can look like huge butterflies.

Artemisia lactiflora White mugwort

Thin plumes of creamy white flowers and deeply cut green leaves. Look out for the variegated variety. The undersides of the green and white leaves are silver-grey, as are the flower spikes.

Aruncus sylvester (*A. dioicus*, *Spiraea aruncus*) Goat's beard

The emerging light green leaves are a fantastic shape. The stately white plumes should be picked at all stages of development, particularly at the moment they are turning white. Allow to relax a little before pressing. The miniature variety is even more attractive, with deeply cut, darker leaves.

Aster novi-belgii Michaelmas daisy

In spite of their thick backs, darker colours and even sprays can be successfully pressed.

Astilbe × arendsii

Press the plume-like heads of tiny flowers, which can be white, pink or red, the latter turning a good brown. Allow some to relax for an hour to create curves.

Astrantia major Masterwort

A star-like flower with stamens like a pincushion. Colours range from cream with green markings to deep pink. The reverse sides are equally attractive. Press buds as well. A good subject for spraying with gold.

Bellis perennis Daisy

The common name is derived from 'day's eye', because the flowers close in the evening and open again in the morning. All garden varieties press well and so do the buds. Look out for greenfly.

Chearophyllum hirsutum roseum Chervil

A rare form, like cow parsley, with lilac-pink umbels. Press florets, whole heads and immature heads with a little stalk. The leaves are larger and denser than those of cow parsley.

Convallaria majalis Lily-of-the-valley

Changes to deep cream and is rather juicy, so press gently with old tissue before pressing whole sprays and a few overlapping bells separately.

Crocosimia Montbretia

Press the small, budded shoots, leaving one or two open flowers on each stem. Press single flowers. All shades stay true.

Delphinium elatum Delphinium

Stately flowers in many colours. All the blues keep their colour well, but white petals become a dirty grey, and pink ones turn a dull mauve. Pick a few flowers from the base of each stem as they come out.

Dianthus Carnation

Cut the flowers just above where the stalk joins the calyx. Squeeze gently to remove the swollen seed pod with the point of scissors before pressing the whole. With buds, use sharp-pointed scissors to clip the calyx from the flower end, cutting halfway through the stalk. Repeat on the other side. Ease gently apart and carefully remove the seed pod. Pull the bud apart, keeping all petal bases within the calyx. Press the two halves.

Dicentra spectabilis alba

This white form presses to a creamy colour, and when it is gently pulled apart resembles a Dutchman dancing. You can have fun with this one.

Doronicum austriacum Leopard's bane

Bright yellow, daisy-like flowers resembling sunrays, 5–6cm (2–2½in) in diameter. They keep their colour.

Epimedium perralderianum Bishop's hat

The little flower sprays should be picked in bud when they have a nice bend at the top. There is not much colour, but the shape is good. The leaves are useful at all stages of development.

Erica and *Calluna* Heather

Press well-flowered stalks of all colours, including white, and also individual florets for miniature designs.

Geranium grandiflorum (*G. himalayensis*)

The bluish-purple flowers are very delicate and some lose their colour. The deep pink-veined varieties, most with black centres, are reliable. Buds and leaves are useful.

Geum chiloense (*G. quellyon*)

Bowl-shaped flowers in bright shades of red, orange and yellow, about 4cm (1½in) across. The red changes to mahogany but is still attractive enough to make it worth pressing.

Gypsophila paniculata Gypsophila, baby's breath

The double form can be pink or white. Press whole sprays, and, if you have time, the little flowers, which resemble tiny powder puffs.

Helleborus foetidus

Greeny-yellow, cup-shaped flowers. Remove the hard stamens, leaving the anthers. Do not bother with buds.

Helleborus niger Christmas rose

The white form should be given some protection from the elements and plenty of slug pellets. Pick flowers just before they open completely, nick out the hard centre stamens and ease flat with your fingers. Buds and leaves should also be pressed. Place one flower on top of another, and put only a dab of adhesive on the centre back because the petals become transparent if they are glued down.

Heuchera sanguinea Coral bells

Pick whole stalks and remove overlapping bells.

Parochetus communis Shamrock pea

Bright, clover-like leaves with vivid blue flowers like miniature sweet peas. These turn a steely blue after pressing.

Phlox paniculata

Use the bi-coloured varieties and press single flowers. The paler shades lose their colour in the press.

Polygonum affine Knotweed

The flower spikes start off deep crimson, turning to pale pink as they mature. After the spike has been pressed, the tiny flowers can be pulled off with a 'stalk' for use in miniature designs.

Phygelius capensis Cape fuchsia
The panicles of flowers are tubular and slightly curved, and they always seem to be full of water. Squeeze out any moisture before pressing.

Potentilla Cinquefoil
Strawberry-like flowers and foliage in many shades, ranging from deep red (which presses deep crimson) to pinks and yellows. Pick before midday or the petals will fall off. They are heart-shaped and can be used for romantic designs. The centres are star-like.

Primula Polyanthus
The yellow shades stay true, but red changes to deep brown, blue to deep navy blue, and pink to purple. The small, gold-edged, gold-centred brown variety presses excellently.

Solidago canadensis Golden rod
Bright yellow, feathery plumes. Pull off some of the lower plumelets with an attached leaf. They usually have a nice curve, but lose some of the bright colour when pressed.

Viola odorata Violet
Treat the flowers in silica gel crystals before pressing, otherwise all the colour goes. Press the heart-shaped leaves, especially the very dark ones.

Viola × wittrockiana
Every shape, shade and size can be pressed, but only the deeper shades keep their colour for any length of time. Snip off the stalks as close as possible to the flowers. Do not press pansies that look cross!

Alpine and Rock Garden Flowers

What a delight an alpine garden can be. Here is everything in miniature, popping up all through the year. Most alpines benefit from a good trim from time to time and never seem to resent having their best flowers and leaves snipped off. If you can, mulch with gravel — the flowers will be cleaner and free from slugs, which like them too.

Acaena glauca New Zealand burr
Tiny, silvery blue foliage. This does very well for miniature work because the leaves resemble tiny rose leaves.

Aethionema 'Warley Rose'
Deep pink heads, like small candytuft, turn a bright purple after pressing.

Ajuga reptans Bugle
The dark wine red leaves and blue spikes both press and keep their colour well.

Alchemilla alpina Alpine lady's mantle
A fantastic plant for pressing: the green, palmate leaves have silver edges and backs like silver velvet. The 15cm (6in) long stems of rather insignificant flowers should be pressed whole to create light, airy spikes.

Alyssum saxatile (*Aurina saxatilis*)
Gold, well-branched heads of flowers. Press whole sprays, which you can divide as required after pressing.

Arabis caucasica
Small white flowers and grey leaves are borne on grey stems. Press sprays as well as individual flowers. The variegated variety is even more attractive.

Aubrietia deltoidea
Cut sprays from the larger, dark purple varieties. Remove any overlapping or dying flowers before pressing leaves and buds.

Cerastium tomentosum Snow-in-summer
White, cup-shaped flowers with useful silver-grey, narrow leaves. Pick sprays with at least one fully open flower.

Geum montanum Mountain avens
Golden yellow, small flowers are followed by fluffy seed-heads. Both can be used successfully.

Helianthemum Rock rose
Flowers must be picked early in the day or the very thin petals will fall. Deep pinks and bright yellows are best; orange and red will turn brick-coloured.

Lithospermum diffusum (*Lithodora diffusa*)
Bright blue, like tiny gentians, these funnel-shaped flowers should be split into two before pressing.

Nierembergia repens
The 2.5cm (1in) wide white flowers are always useful to have.

Saxifraga × urbium London pride
Pick off the tiny pink flowers as they bloom. This is time-consuming and delicate work but is worth every minute because they become miniature butterflies with beautiful markings. The dark stalks and pink buds can be pressed as small sprays.

Sisyrinchium idahoense album 'May Snow'
Iris-like leaves with white, star-shaped flowers, which stay white.

Verbena peruviana
Many colours, the usual one being scarlet, which presses crimson. The variety 'Carousel' has purple and white striped flowers. Press whole heads and a few individual florets for miniature work.

Veronica teucrium (*V. autriaca* subsp. *teucrium*) Speedwell
This is the only speedwell worth pressing. The bright blue spikes retain some colour, unlike the wild species. Press whole spikes.

Bulbs

It never ceases to amaze me that such marvellous flowers come from something that looks like an old onion. What is more, they come up year after year, often increasing themselves, from 15cm (6in) underground, with no help from you and me. It does help, though, if you can give them a foliar feed when they have flowered. It is worth purchasing good bulbs in the first place, and they will reward you for many seasons to come.

Chionodoxa luciliae (*C. forbesii*)
These are not very satisfactory as they

lose so much of their beautiful blue colour in the press. Use scillas instead.

Crocus tommasinianus
Open them up to reveal the inner throat and stamens. The make a good fan or a base for a design.

Freesia Hybrids
Slit the blooms lengthways. Find ones with good markings. The end of the stalk may be pressed with some buds still attached.

Galanthus nivalis Snowdrop
Press some whole stalks after removing the juice. The double flowers of the variety 'Flore Pleno' should be pressed separately, opening them out to reveal their green-striped centres with flashes of orange.

Hyacinthus orientalis Hyacinth
Slice down each bell lengthways. Remove the juicy stamens from the centre. The brighter colours keep well.

Leucojum aestivum Summer snowflake
Like tall snowdrops, but with green tips to the petals. Press whole stalks, which have three or four flowers, but squeeze out the juice first.

Muscari armeniacum Grape hyacinth
The beautifully blue, densely packed flower-heads can be pressed successfully provided that most of the moisture is removed. Place them between old tissues and flatten them gently with an iron, changing the tissues once or twice before placing the flowers between clean tissues in the press.

Narcissus Daffodil
Use the brighter yellow varieties, especially those with flame-coloured cups. Slice the whole flower, trumpet and all, and press out any moisture before placing in the press flat. The miniature, jonquil-types can be pressed successfully, and there is no need to clip the cup unless it is very large — in which case it is not worth pressing.

Nerine bowdenii
Press single flowers as they bloom, carefully removing them from the plant and cutting off most of the calyx Dab the end well as they can be

sticky. Press sideways, and use two to make a 'ribbon bow'.

Ornithogalum thyroides
Chincherinchee
The flowers open continually on the stalk for weeks. Pick or cut off most of the hard calyx. Dab with tissue before pressing. Cut in half, they can be fairies' wings — very ethereal.

Scilla siberica Siberian squill
Pick whole stalks of this vivid blue flower and squeeze out the juice from the stalks before pressing. A good substitute for bluebells.

Shrubs

Not many people think of shrubs when they are contemplating pressing flowers, but they are a great source of foliage. Most evergreen leaves keep their colour well and so are reliable for use in pictures. The flowers on some shrubs are a bonus, and those listed here give good results when pressed.

Berberis thunbergii 'Rose Glow'
Deep pink leaves with white marbling, which keep their colour. Press tips about 20cm (8in) long as well as single, larger leaves.

Caryopteris clandonenesis
Grey-green aromatic leaves with soft blue, tubular flowers. Press sprays of these with the leaves.

Ceanothus
The shiny evergreen leaves are useful for backgrounds. The blue flowers grow at the tips in thimble-like clusters. Choose the brightest blue and press in sprays.

Ceratostigma willmottianum
The terminal clusters of bright blue flowers should be pressed intact. Green leaves become tinged with yellow after pressing.

Chimonanthus praecox (*C. fragrans*)
Wintersweet
Cup-shaped flowers with creamy yellow petals and shorter, purple inner

petals. Ease them out flat to press. They are heavily scented, which is a bonus because the fragrance lingers.

Cistus Rock rose
The single pink flowers must be picked early as they drop their petals after 3–4 hours.

Cytisus Broom
Press the bi-coloured, pea-like flowers and an occasional tip of the branches.

Elaeagnus pungens 'Maculata'
The green and gold, rather tough leaves are evergreen and give good, lasting colour for backgrounds.

Forsythia
Press the yellow flowers singly. Although they can lose their colour, they retain their pretty shape.

Fuchsia magellanica Lady's eardrops
The small flowers keep their colour better and they can be pressed with a stem of leaves, which looks more natural. If you use one of the larger varieties, slice the flowers in half and carefully ease out the juice before pressing. The stamens make wonderful antennae for butterflies. Look out for the variety 'Versicolor'.

Garrya elliptica Silk-tassel bush
Pick the long, grey catkins when they are soft and swinging but before the pollen drops. They can also be picked with one of two leaves and pressed as a pendulous spray of drooping catkins.

Genista Broom
One of the brooms, with the typical yellow, pea-like flowers. Pick and press the flowers separately.

Hamamelis japonica
Japanese witch hazel
Spidery yellow flowers, flushed with red or purple at the base, have a strong, lingering scent.

Hebe
The racemes of varying lengths and colours can be used as long as they are completely dry. Change the pressing paper after two days for best results.

Hibiscus syriacus
Large flowers in a range of colours.

'Dorothy Crane', white flowers with deep red centres, and 'Blue Bird' both press well for large designs. Use the flowers double to give extra depth.

Hydrangea macrophylla
Press individual florets of all colours, including the skeletonized florets that have dried on the bush.

Hypericum St John's Wort
The 5cm (2in) wide yellow, cup-shaped flowers press well for larger designs.

Kerria japonica 'Pleniflora' Jew's mallow, Bachelor's buttons
Little orange-yellow buttons of flowers, 2.5–5cm (1–2in) across.

Lavandula Lavender
Pick well-flowered spikes before they become too dry. These retain their scent for years and, with a Nerine 'bow' make a delightful card.

Leycesteria formosa Himalayan honeysuckle
Greeny bracts, later turning claret coloured, can be used, but best of all are the newly emerging pointed leaves. Pick tip shoots and single, curving leaves.

Myrtus Myrtle
Tiny, white, scented flowers with prominent stamens. These flowers are lovely for miniature work. Also press the tips of shoots of glossy green leaves, which keep their colour.

Neillia thibetica (N. longiracemosa)
Pretty, veined, three-lobed leaves with little semi-pendent trails of rosy-pink flowers. Pick and press these as a spray.

Perovskia atriplicifolia
Grey-green, coarsely toothed leaves with long panicles of insignificant blue flowers. Pick these as a spike and press the leaves separately.

Philadelphus coronarius Mock orange
Sweetly scented white flowers. The small double varieties are best for pressing. They should be picked as a spray when they first open because the petals disintegrate very quickly.

Potentilla fruticosa
Flowers, 2.5cm (1in) across, in yellow, pink and white or red and orange according to variety. Very useful and easy to press if picked early in the day, otherwise the petals drop. Pick a few of the new, dark green leaves.

Rosa Rose
Press all small roses whole and also single, larger flowers, cutting off the calyx as close to the flower as possible. Larger double roses may be dismantled and the petals only pressed — use poppy or hellebore stamens as centres when re-assembling. Slice each bud stem in two as far as the calyx, then pull gently apart, which gives a soft outline to the bud. The purplish leaves and shoots of Rosa rubrifolia (R. glauca) press very well. Other rose leaves lose their colour when exposed to light.

Sambucus nigra laciniata Common elder
The deeply cut leaves are like large ferns.

Sambucus racemosa 'Plumosa Aurea' Red-berried elder
The elder is so useful — finely toothed leaves, bronze-green at first then turning yellow. They turn a beautiful rich brown after pressing.

Spiraea japonica 'Goldflame'
Press new shoots and leaves and, later, those with attractive markings. Pick some shoots, removing covering leaves and pressing these separately. Fluffy heads of star-like, rose-coloured flowers are a bonus, but the foliage is more important.

Weigela florida 'Variegata'
This variety has green and white leaves, which are inclined to darken in the press but nevertheless have a good shape. Do not bother to press the flowers.

Trees

Trees can produce foliage of all different shapes and shades. Select only those leaves that are perfect — there are usually plenty to choose from. Some, such as ash and beech, will completely change colour in the press. Most are listed for their foliage, although some have flowers that can be used.

Acacia dealbata Mimosa
Press sprays after removing any overlapping flowers. Press the little yellow powder-puff balls separately. The fern-like leaves shed their needles very easily.

Acer pseudoplanatus Sycamore
The varieties 'Brilliantissimum' and 'Prinz Handjery' are worth looking out for. The leaves open peachy pink, turning pale green before darkening. Press young leaves, which will become greeny gold. They are a lovely shape.

Chamaecyparis, Cupressus, Juniperus and Thuja Conifers
All the leaves will press. Pick small, young shoots, preferably with gold or silver highlights.

Fagus sylvatica Common beech
Pick very young shoots and remove overlapping leaves, pressing them separately. The more mature the leaves, the darker they become when pressed.

Fraxinus excelsior Common ash
The new, dark green leaves at the tips of branches are identical, which is useful when you are balancing a design. The leaves become black when pressed.

Laburnum anagyroides Common laburnum, Golden chain
The yellow racemes drip with gold flowers, which can be used to create small butterflies.

Prunus 'Kanzan' Cherry
Double pink flowers, which should be pressed when just open or they will fall apart.

Rhus typhina Stag's horn sumach
The deeply cut leaves of this variety can be pressed at all stages of growth, from the new, hardly formed green leaves to the brilliant red and yellow

ones of autumn. Pick these before they fall and pull the larger leaves into leaflets before pressing.

Climbers

All the climbers listed here have something that can be used, and some of them have more than one asset. Take care when you pick leaves or shoots that the leading tip is left until it has reached the height you want. Pinch out and use side shoots, because more will appear.

Bougainvillaea spectabilis
Bright cerise bracts are carried in threes. Separate before pressing. Each one will have a stamen attached.

Cobaea scandens Cathedral bells, Cup and saucer vine
Use the fine, curling tendrils and dark green leaves, which fade to olive.

Eccremocarpus scaber
Chilean glory flower, Glory vine
The tubular orange flowers are not a good shape for pressing. The leaves, stalks and tendril all press jet black. Placed on a pale background they look stunning.

Clematis
The new young tips and leaves of the wild clematis should be allowed to become limp for an hour or so, then press in curves. The stalks become dark and touched with silver. Pick the little grey buds as they are just opening. Slightly spread them apart when pressing to reveal the centres of silky, silver hair, which shine and lighten any design. Press the larger flowers of the garden varieties complete with their fluffy centres. The seed-heads also press well.

Hedera canariensis Canary Island ivy
The variegated variety 'Gloire de Marengo' has silvery leaves. The smaller the ivy, the better it is for pressing purposes.

Hedera helix Ivy
Grow the variety 'Glacier' in a pot.

The leaves will keep their creamy markings if picked before maturity.

Humulus lupulus Hop
Try to find the young, deep green, pointed leaves. The mature ones tend to lose their shape and colour.

Jasminum nudiflorum Winter jasmine
Small yellow flowers on almost leafless shoots. Press the whole shoot for best results.

Jasminum officinale
Common jasmine, Jessamine
Although the white flowers turn pale brown, the leaves and tips of shoots are very useful. Let them relax a little before pressing.

Lonicera Honeysuckle
The best way to press this satisfactorily is to take it apart, pressing each petal separately, then to re-assemble it in your design. Sometimes it is worth the trouble, so press a few in case you need them.

Parthenocissus henryana
Virginia creeper
Pick and press some of the new leaves and shoots, which are pale green. Later they turn from pink to bright scarlet, and that colour stays true for years.

Passiflora caerulea Blue passion flower, Common passion flower
Wonderful dramatic flowers. The stamens and stalked ovaries must be carefully removed and pressed separately. The petals turn to creamy green, but the blue corona keeps most of its colour. Dab the centre well before pressing, because moisture seems to gather there. The young leaves and the shoots, with their curling tendrils, are immensely valuable because they keep their dark green colour.

Polygonum baldschuanicum
Mile-a-minute plant, Russian vine
White flowers, tinged with pink on sprays, which should be pressed whole after relaxing them a little so that the stems fall into curves. Do not press

mature flowers, as they fall off the stems.

Wild Flowers

Some wild flowers are protected by law and must not be picked, so it is as well to check before you set out with your jars, plastic bags and scissors. In any case, never take more than one or two flowers from each plant, leaving some to seed themselves. *Never, never* pull up the roots. Many wild flowers can be grown in your own gardens, and packets of seeds are available. The flowers that follow were not protected at the time of writing.

Aegopodium podagraria Ground elder
Pick the umbels, which are similar to those of cow parsley but green and rather smaller.

Aethusa synapium Fool's parsley
The florets are whiter and crisper than those of cow parsley, with little 'whiskers'. They are inclined to drop after a day or two. Just tap the umbel to make sure. The dark green leaves are finely cut. Pick young shoots as well and press whole.

Anemone nemorosa Windflower, Wood anemone
If you cannot press these immediately after picking, the flowers will close up. Placed in a vase, they will open up again quite quickly. Use the five-lobed, dark green leaves and also the sprays of the leaves with a flower or bud attached.

Anthemis sancti-johannis Camomile, Dog fennel
This can be a garden flower but is often found growing wild. The very satisfactory yellow daisy keeps its colour well, but it has a bulky calyx and needs pressing hard.

Anthriscus sylvestris Cow parsley
The most useful of all wild flowers. Press individual florets; whole heads when you are getting tired; small immature heads; and leaves, both

young and old. You will find a use for all of them.

Anthyllis vulneraria Kidney vetch, Lady's fingers

The pointed leaves and shoots are greenish-grey, with flowers emerging from a thick tuft. Remove most of this, leaving just the yellow tubular flowers surrounded by a coronet of small leaves. Press larger leaves separately.

Bellis perennis Daisy

The flowers can close up if picked after midday. You will need plenty of buds, so this is not a total disaster. Watch for greenfly on pink-tipped flowers.

Brassica napus Rape, Cole

The little yellow flowers are bright and cheerful. Press whole heads and single florets if you have time. Upside down, they resemble little bells.

Cardamine pratensis Cuckoo flowers, Lady's smock

A pale mauve head of flowers. Use on a dark background.

Chaerophyllum temulentum Rough chervil

If possible, pick the foamy flowers with a young leaf or two. The leaves seem thicker and more attractive than cow parsley, and they press very well, keeping their good shape.

Cicuta virosa Cowbane

Found near streams and ditches, this looks like a denser cow parsley.

Crataegus monogyna Hawthorn

Press a few single flowers. They are fiddly to work with but are useful, tiny pink or white flowers with perfect little stamens.

Cruciata laevipes Crosswort

Tiny yellow flowers grow all the way up the stem. Use whole stems for jet black results.

Cymbalaria muralis Ivy-leaved toadflax

Press trailing stems. They will turn almost black.

Daucus carota Wild carrot, Sea carrot

Usually white umbels, which turn pink if there is a cuckoo spit at home. The

pink are the most attractive, so cut with a stalk, rinse the offender out and stand in a jar of water for 24 hours to dry before pressing.

Epilobium angustifolium Rosebay willowherb

The pinkish-purple flowers resemble butterflies when pressed — they even have bodies. Later, the silky, curved seed cases can be used in many ways.

Filipendula ulmaria Meadowsweet

The deep green, pointed leaves have a delightful grey underside. The fluffy flower-heads are butter-cream in colour and should be pressed when there are still a few buds on the spray. Tap them over a piece of paper to dislodge any mites.

Fumaria officinalis Common fumitory

This is included because of its delicate leaf sprays, which form interesting shapes. Remove the flower stalks before pressing.

Galeobdolon argentatum 'Variegatum' Dead nettle

The leaves change colour throughout the year, sometimes acquiring an almost silver appearance in the colder months.

Galium verum Lady's bedstraw

Spiky leaflets with small yellow flowers at the tips. The whole spray presses black.

Geranium robertianum Herb-robert

Insignificant flowers, but the delicate lacy leaves are a joy, and they change colour all year, from green to red.

Geum rivale Water avens

Nodding, rosy-red to brick-red, single flowers with wine red stems. Two or three buds emerge from the axils, and the leaves are very pointed. The garden form is larger but no less attractive.

Heracleum mantegazzianum Giant hogweed

As its Latin name suggests, this is like a huge cow parsley. Press individual flowers, which are sometimes as much as 4cm (1½in) across and look like

lace when pressed. Find those that have turned pink, but you may have to rinse out the cuckoo spit before pressing

Hyacinthoides non-scriptus Bluebell

Pick deep colours with thin stalks. Use silica gel crystals before pressing.

Leucanthemum vulgare Ox-eye daisy

Pick early in the season before they become infested with aphids. Press the buds well.

Linaria vulgaris Toadflax

The tiny yellow flowers resemble tiny antirrhinums. Press each one separately.

Lotus corniculatus Bird's foot trefoil

The young florets are orange, maturing to yellow. Press the whole flower at all stages of development. You can always remove the florets after pressing if you need a single one for a miniature design.

Meconopsis cambrica Welsh poppy

Usually bright yellow, the nodding heads of the buds should be used with the leaves, but they take a long time to dry out.

Oxalis acetosella Wood sorrel

The three-part leaves fold up, but they and the tiny white flowers can be pressed sideways.

Potentilla anserina Silverweed

Useful silver-grey leaves with serrated leaves, which can be separated to make 'seagulls'. Five-petalled flowers, about 12mm (½in) across, are a bonus.

Potentilla erecta Tormentil

Like cinquefoil, but with only four petals and pointed leaves. The trailing variety can take over your garden if you are not careful.

Potentilla reptans Creeping tormentil

Small, five-petalled, bright yellow flowers can be used in small designs.

Potentilla tabernaemontani Spring cinquefoil

Another five-petalled, small, yellow flower with pretty seven-lobed green leaves.

Ranunculus acris Meadow buttercup
Pick all sizes, choosing those with fuller petals. Press open flowers flat and buds when they are showing yellow, removing budlets from the stalks.

Ranunculus ficaria Lesser celandine
Pick the flowers when they are just opening. The centres remain gold and are useful as stamens in make-believe flowers. The petals fade to white.

Sambucus nigra Elder
The foamy white flower-heads turn pale cream. Separate them into manageable sprays, taking out overlapping stalks.

Sanguisorba minor Salad burnet
Small stalks of pretty pinkish-grey or green leaves with rather hard brown flower-heads, like clover. Pick sprays or leaves and flowers before the insignificant petals appear.

Stellaria holostea Greater stitchwort
Press whole spikes with at least one white flower fully open. The sword-like leaves are a good contrast, but they fade easily, so place them on a dark background in your designs.

Vicia cracca Tufted vetch
Small, pinnate leaves. Leave on the little buds, because they take on a most attractive silvery sheen.

Viola lutea Mountain pansy
A quite enchanting miniature yellow pansy with a tiny 'face' — usually smiling!

Viola riviniana Dog violet
These small violets will keep their colour only if they are treated in silica gel crystals before being pressed.

Grasses

Grasses should be picked well before they reach maturity, as they always develop as they are drying. They can be hung up to dry in a dry, warm place without cluttering up your press. When they are fully dry, they can be used in pressed flower designs. Most grasses fade to a pale brown or cream colour, so bear this in mind when you use them.

Apera spica-venti Loose silky-bent, Wind grass
Use as *Deschampsia caespitosa*.

Avena sterilis Animated oats
This is an annual, very similar to field oats, and can be used in large designs.

Brachypodium pinnatum Chalk false-brome, Tor grass
Pointed spikelets on a stem.

Briza maxima Greater quaking grass, Pearl grass
An annual that bears loose panicles of heart-shaped spikelets.

Briza media Common quaking grass, Totter grass
The perennial form has darker spikelets, which look fabulous when sprayed with gold. It can help to place these in a press even after they have dried.

Briza minor Small quaking grass
An annual form, more suitable for miniature work than *B. maxima*.

Bromus diandrus (*Anisantha diandra*) Great brome
Sharp, pointed spikelets.

Cortaderia selloana Pampas grass
Pale, silky, feathery plumes, sometimes with a purple tinge. Pull them to pieces after drying for pressed flower work.

Deschampsia caespitosa Tufted hair-grass, Tussock grass
Dry by standing in a container, which will give you better curves.

Elymus arenarius Lyme-grass
Fine spikes. Press them whole.

Hordeum jubatum Foxtail barley, Squirreltail grass
Graceful, feathery heads. Should be picked when heads are just emerging from the sheath for best results.

Lagurus ovatus Hare's tail
Soft, fur-like heads of great charm. They make you want to stroke them.

Phragmites australis Common reed
Very dark, fluffy heads, which keep their colour.

Stipa pennata Feather grass
Very fine stalks covered with tiny hairs. Most ethereal when used on dark backgrounds.

Ferns

There is an enormous selection of ferns for the flower presser. Only a few have been listed here, most of which can be worked into designs. If space is limited in your press, ferns can be kept almost as satisfactorily in tissue and blotting-paper between two heavy books. Some of the larger varieties can be divided into fronds for easier pressing.

Adiantum capillus-veneris Maidenhair fern
Pretty triangular leaflets, the fronds being carried on black stalks. Pale green, young leaves darken to deep bottle green. Very attractive spores of light to dark brown on the undersides.

Asparagus plumosus (*A. setaceus*) Asparagus fern
Green, feathery foliage, which fades to pale brown very quickly. Pick leaves that are large enough to use as a background for leaf bookmarks.

Asplenium adiantum-nigrum Black spleenwort
Rather hard, leathery leaves. Attractive spores on the backs.

Asplenium ruta-muraria Wall rue
Fronds are irregular and deeply divided. Quite different from the usual fern shape.

Asplenium trichomanes Maidenhair spleenwort
Very small, dark green leaflets with a black stalk. Anything from 4 to 20cm (1½–8in) long. Good for miniature work and presses well, though hard.

Athyrium filix-femina Lady fern
Rather long, pointed leaflets, which
curl a little at the tips.

Athyrium nipponicum (*A. goeringia-num*) Painted fern
The variety 'Pictum' has sage green
fronds variegated with silver-grey.

Cryptogramma crispa Parsley fern
There are two types of deeply cut
leaves to be found growing together.
The sterile leaves are shorter and
wider than the fertile ones.

Cystopteris fragilis Brittle bladder fern
Dark stalks with deeply indented
leaves.

Cystopteris montana
Mountain bladder fern
Long fronds, with the lowest pair of
divisions larger than the others.
Attractively fringed.

Davallia canariensis Hare's foot fern
Deeply cut, mid-green leaflets are
rather tough.

Dryopteris aemula
Hay-scented buckler fern
Long, concave segments, curling
upwards at the tips. Wider leaflets at
the base should be pressed separately.

Dryopteris austiaca Broad buckler fern
Narrowing suddenly at the tip, this
fern is excellent for making 'Christmas
trees'.

Dryopteris carthusiana Narrow buckler
fern
Has paler leaves than the other
buckler ferns.

Dryopteris cristata Crested buckler fern
Narrow fonds that can be used for
'trees'.

Dryopteris filix-mas Male fern
An attractive fern with deep green
leaflets.

Polystichum aculeatum
Hard shield fern
Rather hard, leathery fronds, but a
good bright green.

Polystichum setiferum Soft shield fern
Softer and paler than hard shield fern.

Pteriditum aquilinum Bracken, Brake
The emerging fronds have a nice curl
at the tip. Press them sideways.

Seaweed

Take a plastic bag with you when you
collect seaweed because the fronds
must not be allowed to dry out. Look
for the finer varieties. Rinse the
seaweed thoroughly in cold, fresh
water and sort out the best pieces.
Immerse a sheet of fairly stout paper
in a bowl of clean water. Place some
fronds on the paper and gradually tilt
it as you remove it from the water,
pushing the fronds into shape. Leave
on the paper to dry for 2–3 hours.
Then place between old pieces of
blotting-paper overnight. Next day,
change the blotting-paper and place
in the press. After two days, ease the
seaweed off and place it on the usual
tissue, nappy liner and blotting-paper
combination. Look at it after a day or
two, and if it is sticking, carefully
remove and place it on new tissue.
Believe it or not, this process is worth
it, because seaweed can cleave to the
paper as if it were stuck with glue.
Here are a few to try.

Bootlace weed
Long brown, thong-like fronds.

Ceramium rubrum
Very fine, ethereal pink filaments.

Chanelled wrack
Black seaweed. This will cut to make
delightful 'Lowry' matchstick men.

Red and green dulse
Thin, flat fronds like satin ribbon.

Rhodomela subfusca
Pink, bushy tufts, sometimes with a
hint of green.

Herbs and Vegetables

The herb patch and vegetable garden
can be a source of inspiration, especially for short-term designs. The
green leaves fade to a creamy colour
quite quickly. Vegetables themselves
can be used if thinly sliced and
pressed with care, but they have little
charm unless they are used for a
specific purpose such as a kitchen
design.

Anthriscus cerefolium Chervil
A useful, bright green, ferny leaf.
Delicate umbels of white flowers
should be picked before they are too
mature or they scatter their petals.

Artemisia absinthium Wormwood
Silky, serrated silver-grey leaves. All
the artemisias are of value for flower
pressers.

Borago officinalis Borage
Bright blue, five-petalled, star-shaped
flowers. Remove the calyx before
pressing and use two or three because
the petals are very thin.

Carum carvi Caraway
Finely cut, ferny leaves similar to
carrot leaves.

Daucus carota Carrot
Well worth growing, even if you don't
like eating them, just for the leaves.
Nip off one or two from each carrot,
and they won't know.

Foeniculum vulgare Fennel
Thread-like, blue-green leaves. The
bronze variety has, well, bronze leaves.
All carry umbels of golden flowers.
Press these as you would cow parsley:
some flat heads, some individual
flowers (which are useful for lighting
up autumnal designs), and the feathery
leaves in small, well-filled sprays.

Hyssopus officinalis Hyssop
Blue terminal flowers on leafy spikes.
Press whole spikes.

Petroselinum crispum Parsley
This is the curled variety, which has a
mossy look. Use the young, bright
green leaves.

Pisum sativum Pea
The tendrils should be carefully
removed when they are just about to
curl. Do not bother to press the
flowers or the leaves.

Ruta graveolens Rue
    Ornamental, lace-like leaves with a blue-grey hue.

Vicia faba Broad bean
    The white and black flowers can be pressed for butterflies. But remember that for every flower you pick, you lose seven or eight beans.

Grey Foliage Plants

These are very useful in pressed flower work. One advantage is that they never fade. When you use them on candles, all grey leaves turn green, and if they fade, they turn back to grey.

Anthemis punctata subsp. *cupaniana*
    A small perennial that spreads like a cushion. The aromatic, grey-green leaves are finely cut, and there are daisy-like flowers.

Pyrethrum ptarmicaeflorum 'Silver Feather'
    Very fine cut leaves. Pick the centre of a leaf spray and press whole, pressing the larger leaves separately.

Santolina chamaecyparissus Cotton lavender
    Finely divided, silver-grey leaves carried on thin stalks. Press whole stalks to give height to a design.

Senecio maritima 'Silver Dust'
    Rather coarse, fern-like foliage with felty white undersides.

Tanacetum haradjanii (*Chrysanthemum haradjanii*)
    Very deeply dissected, small, silver leaves, almost like filigree. Very pretty for small designs.

SUPPLIERS

Framecraft Miniatures Ltd
372–376 Summer Lane
Hockley
Birmingham B19 3QA
(tel: 021 212 0551)

Ireland Needlecraft Pty Ltd
4, 2–4 Keppel Drive
Hallam
Victoria 3803
Australia (tel: 03 702 3222)

Hannelore Kopp
Bayerischer Platz 7
1000 Berlin 30
Germany (tel: 853 9869)

The Embroidery Shop
Greville-Parker
286 Queen Street
Masterton
New Zealand (tel: 6 377 1418)

Ann Starr
8 Avenue des Frenes
B1950 Kraainem
Belgium

Danish Art Needlework
PO Box 442
Lethbridge
Alberta T1J 3ZI
Canada (tel: 403 327 9855)

Sanyei Imports
PO Box 5
Hashima Shi
Gifu 501–62
Japan (0583 92 6532)

Anne Brinkley Designs Inc
761 Palmer Avenue
Holmdel
NJ 97733
USA (tel: 908 787 2011)

Gay Bowles Sales Inc
PO Box 1060
Janesville
WI 53547
USA (608 754 9212)

Dollfus Mieg & Co.
Viale Italia 84
1–20020 Lainate
Milan
Italy

Resin Supplies
Trylon Ltd
Thrift Street
Wollaston
Northants NN9 7QJ
(tel: 0933 664275)

Porcelain
Held of Harrogate
16 Station Parade
Harrogate HG1 1UE
(tel: 0423 504772)

Stationery and Card, etc.
Craft Creations
Units 1–7 Harpers Yard
Ruskin Road
Tottenham
London N17 8NE
(tel: 081-885 2655)

Jewellery Findings
T. H. Findings Ltd
42 Hylton Street
Hockley
Birmingham B18 6HN

Boxes
Atlantic Box & Cartons Ltd
Riverside House
Heron Way
Newham
Truro
Cornwall TR1 2XN
(tel: 0872 71600)

ACKNOWLEDGEMENTS

To the late Arthur Lundhal, of the United States of America, who gave
me the idea of pressing flowers so many years ago.

To Serafina Clarke, my agent, for all her support.

To Angela Byrne, of Creative Framing, Wadebridge.

To Arty-Craft of Wadebridge for materials.

To the many friends who have given me encouragement in writing this
book, particularly Joan Nunn, Jenni Milne, and Jackie Smith.

Lastly, but by no means least, David Porteous, for his boundless
enthusiasm, which has made it all possible.

DAVID PORTEOUS ART & CRAFT BOOKS

Flower Painting Paul Riley
Watercolour Landscapes Paul Riley
The Dough Book Tone Bergli Joner
Fun Dough Brenda Porteous
Paperworks Dette Kim
Wooden Toys Ingvar Nielsen
Papier Mâché Lone Halse
Pressed Flowers Pamela Le Bailly
Silhouettes in Cross Stitch Julie Hasler
Cats: A Cross Stitch Alphabet Julie Hasler
Gift Boxes Claus Zimba Dalby
Decorative Boxes Susanne Kløjgård
Paper Craft Dette Kim
Fairytale Doughcraft Anne Skødt
Dolls' Clothes Mette Jørgensen